# Life With a Legend

### BY

### LARRY HINSON

Published By
Sow the Seed Ministries

Life With A Legend
© 2004 by Larry Hinson
Published by Sow The Seed Ministries
P.O. Box 529
White House, TN 37188
1-888-577-1929
Printed in the United States of America

Some names have been changed to protect identity.

*All rights reserved.* No part of this publication may be reproduced, stored in a retrieval system, or transmitted, in any form or by means, electronic, mechanical, photocopying, recording, or otherwise, without the prior written permission of the publisher.

White House, TN

# TABLE OF CONTENTS

Dedications ..................................................................5
Acknowledgements .......................................................5
Preface .........................................................................7
Big Brother ..................................................................11
I See The Devil ...........................................................33
Now That's Entertainment ..........................................55
Goodbye World, Goodbye ..........................................65
A Promise To Be Number One ...................................73
Nightmare On Zoe Street ............................................83
A Taste Of The Big Time ..........................................103
The Big Move ............................................................119
Lights, Cameras, Action ............................................129
A Time Of Discovery .................................................141
The Nation's Number One Group .............................149
Joseph And His Brothers ..........................................157
A Call To Pastor ........................................................163
The Hinsons Make A Come Back .............................171
The Last Performance ...............................................175
The Legend Has Passed ...........................................179
Picture Album ............................................................189

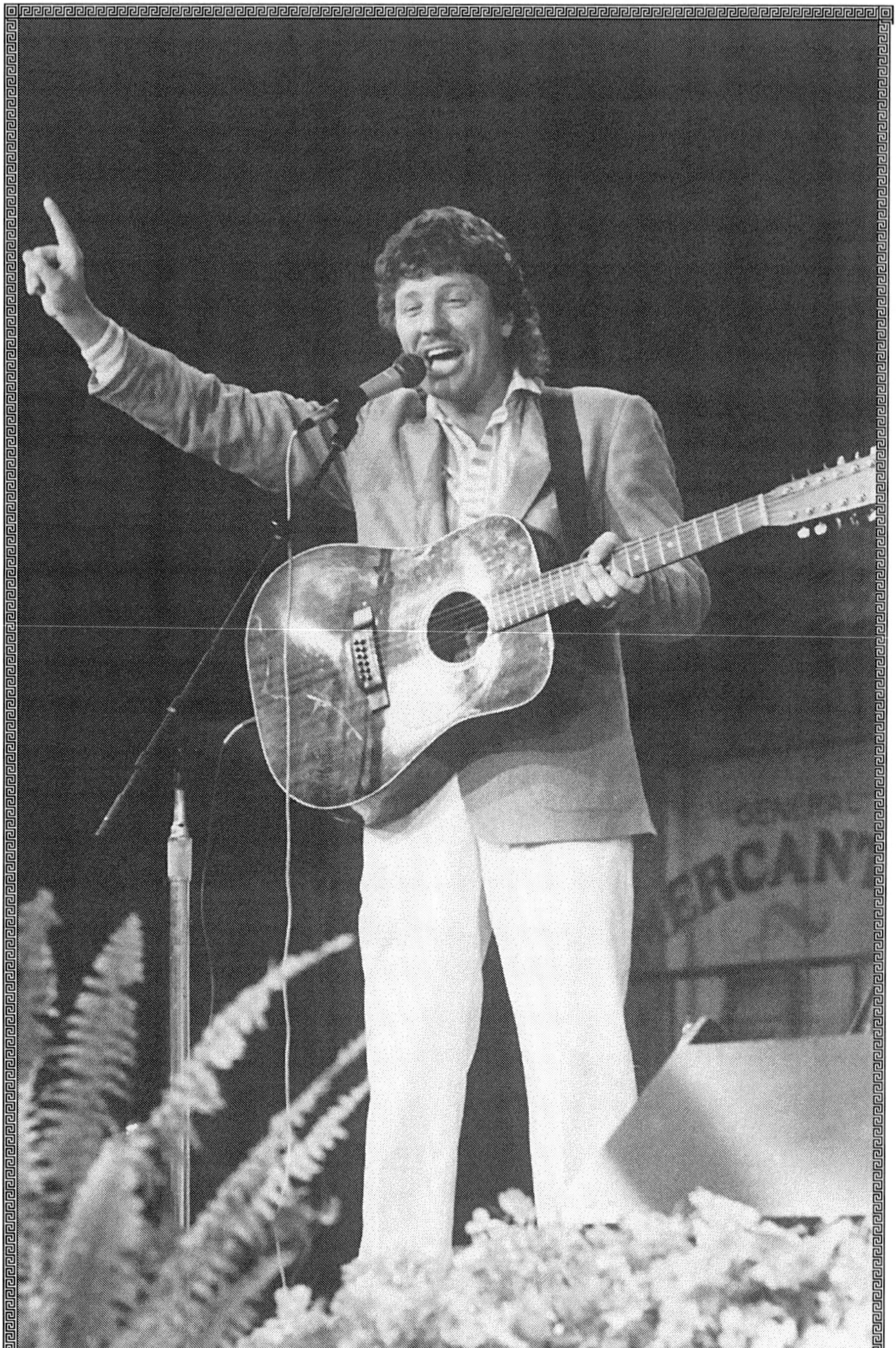

# DEDICATIONS

To my mother Stella, who first knew Kenny's love and lost her baby boy on July 27, 1995. Remember, "But we do not want you to be uninformed brethren about those who are asleep, so that you will not grieve as the rest who have no hope. For if we believe that Jesus died and rose again, even so God will bring with Him those who have fallen asleep in Jesus." I Th. 4:13-14. (NASU.)

To Amanda and Weston, who were forced to finish their childhood without their father's love and will never know the advice and comfort that, only a dad can share. Don't forget I love you and I'll do my very best to be here for you! Remember to do the work of the Lord and always serve Jesus so that you may see your dad again face to face someday.

# ACKNOWLEDGEMENTS

First I would like to say thank you to my dear friends Roy and Ann Chapman and Trey and Tammy Sanford. Without your contributions and assistance, this book would not have been possible. You were always loved and cherished by Kenny and I know you loved him deeply!

To Yvonne, Mama, and my old friend Duane Guffy, thanks for the additional photographs, you really helped to add great emphasis to the book.

To my oldest son Jay for his graphic design on the cover, you did an excellent job!

To all my children Jay, Lyndi and Matthew, for enduring the many hours of my absence during our usual times together, thank you for your understanding and patience. Thanks also for more or less tiptoeing past my office door each day for the past several months.

Above all, thank you to my lifelong friend and sweetheart, Jana I appreciate your cooperation and assistance in so many areas I could never name them all. I thank you for the many times you have driven for me on long trips while I typed away on my lap top and the countless nights you went to bed alone, as I continued working on this biography into the wee hours of the morning.

Thanks to all of you who read this story and loved Kenny so very much, thanks for helping to keep his memory and legacy alive!

**Larry**

# PREFACE

Kenneth Duane Hinson, was born at the Santa Cruz County Hospital in Santa Cruz, California, on October seventeenth, nineteen fifty three. He was the seventh child of eight children that were born to Cecil and Stella Hinson. At the time of his birth, the Hinsons lived at 30b Hawthorne Road in Watsonville.

Almost immediately after his birth, Kenny suffered from anemia. By the time he was a toddler, he was struggling to overcome bronchitis that would leave his lungs permanently damaged with scar tissue. Kenny would spend a great portion of his early life, battling with one sickness after another.

Kenny's parents had a firm confidence in the Biblical principles of prayer and a strong belief in the power of faith. They possessed every reason to expect that God would ultimately alter the frail condition of Kenny's body and bring to him the long awaited benefits of divine healing. Eventually, Kenny's health would improve and by his early teens, Kenny would go on to develop into a strong and healthy young boy.

It was during those early years of his life that Kenny would discover both persistence and courage, for everything he would desire to receive from God.

Being raised in a Christian home and trained up under his parents' pastoral, Kenny was exposed early on to both the preaching of the word and gospel singing.

No doubt Kenny received his experience in scriptural knowledge from his father, however it was unquestionably his mother that helped to focus his attention on singing and playing instruments.

Mom started Kenny's lessons, by simply showing Kenny how to place his small fingers on the strings of an old box guitar. Teaching him how to form the chords comprised of some primary keys, was all that was necessary to spark the divine talent he possessed. Although mom attempted to expose Kenny to the joys of other instruments as well, the guitar soon became Kenny's instrument of choice. No one ever had to force Kenny to practice playing his guitar. In fact, often he had to be dissuaded from practicing, due to its irritating effects on the rest of the family.

Kenny's hard work and practice inevitably paid off and by the tender age of fifteen, Kenny was thrust into the world of singing along side the heavy weights of the southern gospel music industry.

With a love for the down home country sounds of such country music giants as "Merle Haggard" and a genuine passion for the old conventional gospel songs of yester year, Kenny naturally began forming a style of music all his own.

As the years went by and Kenny's personal following began to increase, the gospel music industry had no choice but to recognize the new style of music that Kenny had developed.

By 1976, Kenny was voted "Favorite Lead Vocalists," by the "Singing News Fan Awards." This would be only one of many awards to follow, in the comparatively short music career of Kenny Hinson. However, there is no doubt that Kenny would ultimately help to reshape the entire field of southern gospel music and go on to become one of the most celebrated voices ever to sing on a gospel music stage.

Though many have and will attempt to copy his unique sound, there will never be another Kenny Hinson. Yet without question, he has left an indelible mark on all who have heard him sing, or known him personally.

True to his need for perfection, Kenny has long since moved away to a more perfect place and yet his legendary sounds remain with us today, through the means of modern recordings.

It is my personal desire to help the reader realize both the man as well as the singer, as you go back with me to a time when a legend was being shaped. For this reason, I have chosen to mostly show you Kenny Hinson from behind the stage curtains and away from the gospel music crowds. I wanted to depict him in all his frustrations and fears, as well as both his faith and hopes.

I realize that in my efforts to describe the events portrayed in this biography, some of my memories will most assuredly conflict with those of my siblings and other family members as well. It for this reason that I request them to bear with me in my recollection, with respect to my age, during particular periods of time this writing discusses. I am convinced that no two people have an identical memory, of any single event and therefore ask that they indulge me to that degree.

It is my greatest wish that when you have concluded this peek into the personal life of this gospel music icon that you too truly realize what I have come to know. For a short time, we were genuinely visited by one of God's greatest blessings!

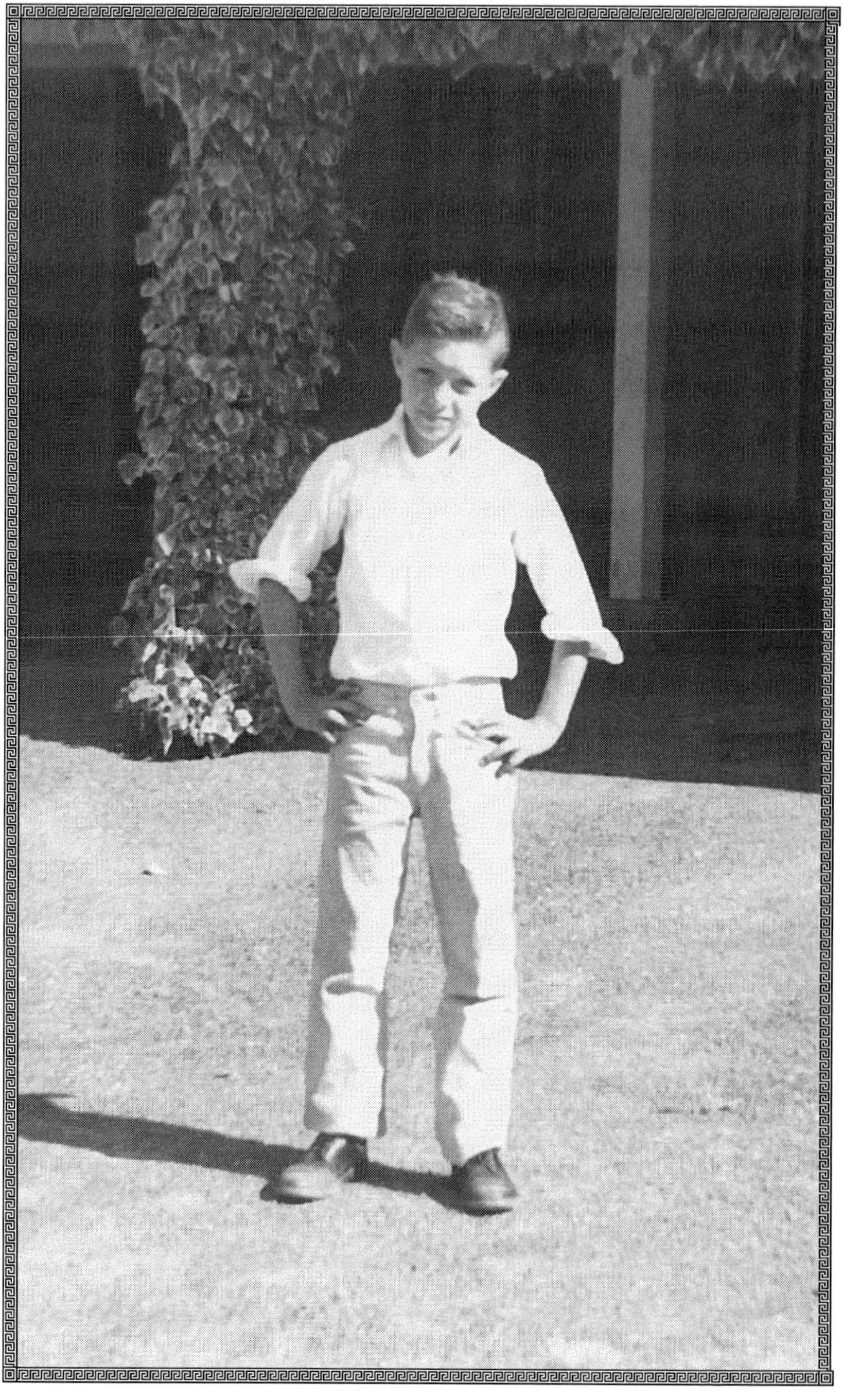

# CHAPTER ONE

## BIG BROTHER

As far back as I can remember my brother Kenny has always been an intricate part of my life. Born October 17, 1953, he was three years my senior. Because Kenny was already eight years old and I was still just five, I remained home most weekday mornings while Kenny went off to school. For my mom and dad, as it was for many people in 1961, kindergarten was not yet a readily accepted concept. For this reason, I was forced to be without Kenny's company for long hours at a time. I can still recall the loneliness I felt inside as I watched him board the big yellow school bus that stopped at the end of the long gravel drive which wound from our house down the grassy slope to where it junctioned with the paved rural two lane. From the big barn shaped house we called home in Aromas, California, I would longingly peer after him through the large bay window in our living room, standing on my tip toes and straining to see over the window sill.

I can still recall the eagerly awaited signal of recognition, the one last wave of acknowledgement Kenny always seemed to throw my direction, just before he climbed aboard the gigantic multi-glassed vehicle. My whole world seemed to temporarily pivot on this small gesture of thoughtfulness. It was, in my way of thinking, the necessary sustenance I required in order to endure the loneliness that rushed into my mind each day only moments after his departure.

I did not see him then as some astonishing singer or view him as a celebrity of any kind. To me, Kenny was virtually one thing and one thing only: big brother. It was during this particular time in my life that I first began to realize the significance of having someone who was in fact both my playmate and my hero. I never had a problem with being "Little Brother," the sidekick, the Tonto to the Lone Ranger. To me, it was just simply neat to be his companion, regardless of what we did together or where we did it.

I was the youngest of eight children and because of the vast differences between my older siblings and myself, it was understandable that they would naturally take less interest in me than Kenny did. The oldest of the eight children in our family was Teddy. After her came Barbara and both of them were already married with children. Third in line and oldest of the boys in our family, was Calvin. After Calvin came Harold and then Ronny. Calvin, Harold and Ronny were all teenagers in 1961 and were deeply involved with their own interests which included best friends and girl friends and for Calvin, the Air Force.

Yvonne, the youngest of the girls and six years my elder, took pleasure in just one thing with regard to me. She liked to dress me up as a little girl and pretend that I was her daughter. Thank God, her particular interests never extended beyond the living room of our house. She did, however, really seemed quite proud of her accomplishments at the time, even showing me off on occasion to our mother as a little girl she had found playing outside! My feminine attire would usually consist of whatever rag tag pile of materials Yvonne might locate at the moment and she took great effort to make certain I was convincing to all in appearance. I, of course, was all boy and wanted no part of that; however, Yvonne often got her way despite my protests, through a simple method of black mail. She would often threaten to make up a story about me being disobedient if I did not cooperate. Then I would be in big trouble with Mom.

Kenny, on the other hand, took an interest in more of the things that I liked. As any young boy raised in the nineteen sixties, I had more of a macho concept when it came to having a fun time. I can still remember the excitement I felt welling up in my chest whenever I heard the screech of the bus brakes, which indicated the return of my playmate. I knew that Kenny was truly my means of escape from Yvonne's strange ideas of having a good time. Kenny would never require me to dress up like some silly little girl and make some grand procession in front of other people. When my hero was home from school, it was time for bikes and tricycles, soldiers, cowboys and Indians.

I don't need to remind you that this was the era of such popular television shows as "Wagon Train," "Bonanza," "Gun Smoke," "Rifle Man" and of course my favorite, "Superman." It was a hero's world at that time in America and we were the product of those days. It seemed like almost all of my imaginative input came from TV or from my big brother Kenny. Kenny seemed to have the method to produce all the really important issues to a five-year-old. Together, we were the original dynamic duo, the first "Batman and Robin."

To make things even better, when our oldest sister Teddy came to visit, she would sometimes bring my nephew Kurt. Kurt was exactly two months older than I was. When the three of us got together, oh, brother! Look out! We made up a special Green Beret division unlike any the world has ever known!

On certain occasions, we turned into the ultimate superheroes whose mission was to save the world from unseen evil forces. With bath towels around our necks held in place by safety pins or clothespins, we flew off to meet dangerous challenges like three caped crusaders, determined to rid the universe of every diabolical foe we encountered. Of course, we had super powers far exceeding those of Spider Man, Thor, The Fantastic Four, or even Superman himself. We always managed to thwart every villain's attempt to overthrow the governments of the world as Triampula, Wizirdo and The Bull.

We knew in our minds that whenever these three sources of ultimate power came together as one unit for the purpose of fighting crime, it was because the world leaders had no doubt reached the end of their military ropes. They obviously found themselves in a desperate position and needed the maximum in strength and unwavering resolve. We were known to those in danger of complete and total annihilation as the last hope for the survival of mankind and the world as they knew it. We were The Revengers to the rescue! With my supernatural strength as Triampula, I was able to carry the complete weight of the entire galaxy in one hand, not to mention being totally impervious to all kinds of weapons, poisons, pain or galactic substances.

When Kurt, The Bull, was on the job, there was absolutely no chance of a villain escaping from his attack. Even the strongest and thickest of barriers could not withstand his charge. Just one butt from his gigantic horns and he broke easily through the hardest matter and anti-matter materials. He was naturally headstrong and sported a hot temper capable of increasing his strength and size far beyond the puny abilities of someone like The Hulk.

As Wizirdo, Kenny held the power of unimaginable magic and could control both time and energy. When we created a scenario Wizirdo should not have been able to escape from, he could simply wave his hand in the air and the scenario no longer existed. Oh, for the ability to still do that today! The contemporary generation will truly never know just what debt of gratitude they owe The Revengers regarding world peace and mere existence for that matter.

Those were the days when Kenny taught me how to disobey our parents. It was he who first convinced me that Mom would never know if we left the front yard long enough to slip off to old man Tucker's place and get our army supplies. Old man Tucker, worked for Lara Scudder, a west coast snack food company that produced our favorite barbecued potato chips. Kenny initially introduced me to such scrumptious delicacies and we simply found it to impossible to resist them. After all, Kenny argued, "Strong armies have to have plenty of food rations." Of course, each time we slipped off to Tucker's house, Kenny always classified it as a Top Secret Operation.

Somehow the enemy, which looking back must have been our mother, seemed to always discover our absence, regardless of our secrecy, we would inevitably wind up in big trouble. I still suspect that one of our older brothers may have worked as a double agent in such cases. Surely they must have noticed us coming back down the hill, brandishing our brightly colored packages. Soon we were under house arrest and forced to occupy our minds with a more permissible act of interest. Mom, however, didn't seem to understand the reasoning behind our deliberate rebellion. Old man Tucker just gave that stuff away to us kids. We didn't need any money, so it was more than we could endure, just standing by while all the other kids headed up the hill to Tucker's. We usually found ourselves in either the front or back yard when that happened, just standing there watching longingly, in the burning Saturday afternoon heat, as the whole neighborhood made the trek up the well beaten path to enjoy those culinary delights. We had nothing to titillate our taste buds, accept the sun-heated water in the rubbery tasting hose that squirted in every direction because of the worn out threading around its connection to the faucet.

Soon after we finally obtained our acquittal, old man Tucker died suddenly and no one seemed to have any reason any longer to climb the hill. We continued, however, to find ways to replenish our army supplies. It was also in Aromas that I first got a taste of homemade vanilla snow cream. That winter in 1961, it snowed in the San Joaquin valley in central California for the very first time in nearly eighty years.

Kenny and I were elated over the experience to begin with but when we discovered the delight of the creamy desert we were thrilled beyond words! Now don't get me wrong, we had often stopped with Mom and Dad at the local Foster's Freeze to eat an ice cream cone. Yet we had never experienced anything so full of the rich vanilla flavor that snow-cream provided.

Kenny and I couldn't get enough of the stuff. Not to mention the excitement of throwing our very first snow balls at one another. The event was so rare for that part of the country that Mom was not about to let the occasion slip away without catching it on film. She got out her old imitation Browning camera and lined us up against the outside of the house for a backdrop. I can still recall watching Kenny laugh hard as water from a melting icicle dripped down the collar of Yvonne's dress. I laughed my head off that day and Yvonne laughed as well. To be quite honest with you, I wasn't altogether sure why Kenny found the dripping icicle so hilarious. But, if my big brother thought it was that funny then so did I.

That same year, we made an unexpected trip to El Paso, Texas, where my Uncle Floyd and Grandma Ida, resided. Floyd was one of Dad's younger siblings and provided their mother with room and board during the last days of her life. Dad was anxious to see his mom, since it had already been several years since his last visit with her. For some strange reason, people didn't seem to visit relatives who lived a long way away like they do today. Perhaps it was the more conservative concept with regard to money still lingering from the Great Depression of the thirties and forties. Or, perhaps it was the pioneer mentality that caused people to travel great distances away from family and never look back. There they would settle to start a new life and basically resolve themselves to the idea that they might never see their loved ones again.

For whatever reasons, people usually adopted the perspective that only a terminal illness or a funeral merited enough purpose for them to make the long journey to see their families. I can still remember my mom and dad loading our car down with pillows and blankets and a variety of items, just to make a trip to the town of Paso Robles. Paso Robles was only about a hundred miles away. Yet that little town seemed an eternity away and we always took too much stuff whenever we went there.

When we discovered that El Paso was several hundred miles away, Kenny and I nearly freaked out. The world just seemed so much larger then. When it came time to go to Texas, to us it felt enormous! You can't even begin to imagine the unnecessary junk we had crammed into our 1956 Chrysler Windsor. Loaded to the hilt, we made the long arduous journey down through Bakersfield and out onto the now famous Route 66.

The temperature didn't vary much in Central California in the early 1960s. For the most part, every summer seemed to stay in the high sixties and low seventies. It was a rarity indeed to experience high seventies then. At least for those of us living within about thirty miles from the coast, there were plenty of cool breezes that blew inland to keep the climate mild enough. Though often overcast, rainy or foggy, we usually preferred the damper weather to the hotter climates experienced just a few miles south of our location. In our neck of the woods, very few people spent money on the luxury of an air conditioner in their house let alone their cars. We were soon to discover, however, that our vehicle was by no means capable of sustaining a moderate atmosphere when inundated with the soaring heat wave that was stretching across the whole of the Mojave Dessert.

The temperatures did not seem to lessen any as we wearily passed through Arizona and New Mexico at a snail's pace. The one single item that brought even the slightest bit of comfort during that long sultry test of endurance, was the lone wash cloth that Mom had carried with us from home. Without that little piece of material, we were convinced we would have no doubt perished soon after our departure from

Aromas. The raggedy patch of cotton provided some cool consolation whenever the heat became too unbearable. Mom had evidently made of few of these trips before and seemed to have the insight to properly prepare. She had literally traveled in a covered wagon as a girl and had often had to endure such hardships for much greater lengths of time. So she sometimes told us stories about her childhood and all the difficulties they had to suffer. I suppose she told us these things in order to help ease our present woes. It didn't seem to help a lot in reality. Within just a few moments of her stories' conclusion, Kenny and I were right back to feeling miserable and complaining again.

Cooling ourselves by wetting the cloth and laying it over our faces only seemed to actually heat things up when the outside temperatures began to rise above one hundred degrees. Two children and one washcloth between us! I was beginning to wonder if mom was really all that prepared for the trip after all.

Soon, World War III broke out in the back of the old Chrysler, over a slightly dampened wash cloth. For hours, the hot sun beat down upon us, and Kenny and I were both sweaty and cranky. To make matters even worse, dad was into the latest fad: preserving the car seat cushions with bubbled plastic seat covers. Not only did the seat covers stick to sweaty skin, they would burn you as well. Finding a place in the back seat where the blistering rays couldn't fry an egg was about as difficult to find as a convenient parking space when you're in a hurry. I got more and more angry by the minute. Kenny simply wouldn't get out of the shaded areas. The way I saw it, Kenny was just too tall! His long legs kept on intruding into my territory. He repeatedly flung them across the imaginary boundary I had drawn with my index finger down the middle of the car seat.

After a while, my tolerance level reached its limit, and I gave him a good swift kick, followed by some lengthy words of warning. I informed him quite loudly about what I would ultimately do to him if he chose to throw his legs on my side again! "Stay off my side, or I'll kick you in the leg again," I chided. Of course, I supported this vehement threat with a minor demonstration of weaponry. As any good show of military strength would demonstrate, I dislodged his foot from its location with a glancing blow from the heel of my tennis shoe. This of course seemed to me to be the necessary method to display the full strength of the impact looming as a consequence of his refusal to comply. I had already decided that the next strategic target would be his shinbone, if he chose to cross that line again.

Unfortunately, the enemy launched a surprise counter attack, landing both his feet simultaneously against my right upper thigh in two powerful strikes just as I was preparing to lock and load. Needless to say, the back seat war was on! Mom and Dad had learned to somewhat tune us out whenever they were engaged in a conversation. Currently they were in a deep discussion about Dad's sick mother. Tuning out two rowdy kids who might just as well be playing as fighting, was certainly not a difficult thing to do after a while. They appeared completely unaware of the seriousness of the altercation and continued to ignore our threatening shouts at one another until we broke into a fierce battle.

Push came quickly to shove and, without question, Kenny was getting the upper hand. That is, until I threw something totally unexpected into the mix. From that day on, it would become my secret weapon whenever it appeared as though I was losing a fight. At the time, however, I really never dreamed it would be effective. Being raised in a Christian home, I believed completely that prayer released divine intervention. For some strange reason, I related wishing and hoping to a type of prayer for God's assistance in any given situation. After all, even at five years old, I knew that God was fully aware of every intent of the heart. Wishing or hoping for Him to intervene on one's behalf would be the same as inviting Him to assist. He would then have no choice but to respond to that person's desires. It was from this somewhat warped concept of prayer that I quite unintentionally launched that secret weapon.

"Are you hoping you'll win?" I blurted out.

"What?" Kenny recoiled in an obvious state of confusion.

"Do you hope that you'll win the fight?" I repeated, this time doing my very best to sound as victimized as possible.

"Hope that I'll win? What are you talking about?" Kenny responded this time with an expression of disbelief on his face. "Of course I hope that I'll win!"

"No fair hoping you'll win," I shouted with an almost sacred timbre.

Kenny's head then snapped back, as if to avoid a sudden smack in the face. With a startled expression, he smugly retorted, "You've lost your mind! What in the world are you talking about?"

I knew exactly what any five-year-old kid about to turn six would know, when it came to hoping. Further more, I was certain that by the time I finished explaining it to him, he too would fully understand the concept and cease his insistence on hoping he'd win. This was a serious matter you see. You didn't just hope whenever you wanted to win some scuffle. No, hoping had to be reserved for much larger issues, like hoping you'd get a certain present for Christmas or hoping Dad would stop for something cold to drink. Those circumstances certainly merited hoping. However, hoping to win a conflict over your little brother was totally unfair.

With the confidence of someone possessing all the scriptural insight of a scholar, I clearly and concisely informed him of the similarity between hoping and prayer. "You can't hope you'll win, because hoping is like praying for help, and it's no fair asking God for help to win." I paused for a moment, staring at him with an inquisitive expression on my face, as if to ask him by the look I was currently exhibiting if he understood the wisdom in my explanation. He stared back at me, as if he was currently witnessing the weirdest thing he had ever seen.

Realizing his inability to grasp the depth of my explanation, I tried to put it as simply as possible. "It's against the Bible to get God to help you beat up your little brother. That's what Cain got in trouble for," I went on to say, suddenly remembering the Sunday school lesson of Cain and Abel.

"You're crazy," Kenny shouted back. "Cain killed Abel, stupid. I'm not trying to kill you yet, I'm just trying to defend myself."

"Oh, yeah?" I replied sarcastically.

"Yeah," Kenny shot back.

"The only reason you've been winning is because you've been hoping. Stop hoping and see what happens," I said as though it was at matter of theological fact. Now I was convinced that no further argument was necessary to drive my point home. Kenny would simply agree, seeing the error of his ways and the kickboxing match could continue, with the inevitable winner being yours truly. For a moment, I was certain it had worked. Kenny remained completely silent at the conclusion of my last statement, and I was sure that his pause indicated his awareness of my being right.

Instead, Kenny reared back and started laughing. "You have lost your mind," Kenny said, doubling over with even more laughter now.

"All right, that's it!" I screamed, with an almost maniac appearance to my face. "You asked for it." Rapid-fire feet strikes, against both his shinbones, seemed to be the solution to this conflict. Negotiations had obviously broken down and there was currently only one option left. I would attack quickly while the enemy was unaware I was coming. I kicked Kenny's now drawn in shin bones as fast as I could. But Kenny just kept laughing harder. When I became aware of the fact that Kenny was not going to stop laughing at me, I resorted to the only recourse I had left in my arsenal: allied forces! I cried for help! I turned and looked in the direction of

Mom, who was still deeply engaged in a conversation with Dad. "Mom, Kenny's laughing at me!" My tone made it sound as if Kenny was committing a repeat offence and it was my duty to report it to her. "He said I've lost my mind." This was ultimately the wrong move on my part. Instead of acquiring the support of the allied forces, I incurred the anger of the superpower driving the car.

"All right you two," Daddy blurted. "You better cut it out right now!" Now I'm not sure how most dads were during the nineteen sixties, however, my dad was a no nonsense kind of guy. Particularly when it came to warnings, my dad played by one set of rules: his. First, you got the initial notice to stop whatever it was that was annoying him. Second, you received a word of caution, informing you of what he would do to you if he should have to tell you again to stop. By the third statement, you were already under attack, and all anyone needed to know was where to send the flowers.

Somehow, Kenny and I had become so engrossed in the onslaught of the battle that we managed to completely ignore the first warning. I thought that surely my cries for help would not go entirely unattended, if I just kept complaining in between attempts to take matters back into my own hands. If I did it through the occasional covert strike against Kenny, while simultaneously continuing my efforts to employ mom's assistance, I would eventually come out on top of the situation.

All at once, Dad cleared his throat in the all too familiar fashion, which usually preceded a stern advisory. Suddenly, he reached up and adjusted the rear view mirror, giving him the maximum range of vision. Before we knew it, we were eyeball to eyeball with the angel of death. Those cold, dark brown eyes, staring back at us through the windshield's little looking glass appeared glazed over with the murderous expression of a madman. We knew it now, just as surely as a man awaiting his execution on death row: We were about to die.

Reflecting back on the moment, I cannot tell you just how truly panic stricken we were when we came face to face that day with the Grim Reaper, however, I can tell you that I remember longing to be quietly sweating to death in the back seat instead. That penetrating look was all it took to make my enemy my friend! We immediately realized that the only way to get out of this sticky situation was to stick together. Perhaps a diversionary tactic would provide the solution, so we quickly started blaming the heat and our unbearable thirst for our actions.

Surprisingly enough, it worked! Finally, Mom came to our rescue. "Cecil," she said compassionately. "These kids our burning up. We're going to have to stop and get something cold to drink." Dad readjusted his mirror back to its usual position, and we breathed a sigh of relief.

Now, perhaps it was because Dad was on some mental time limit or simply because service stations and restaurants were few and far between out there in the desert. Whatever the real reason, we never seemed to stop for anything other than gas and to go to the bathroom. The latter of which nearly required the proverbial act of Congress each time. Dad always argued that soft drinks or "soda water," as Mom and Dad called them, cost money we didn't have to spend. Dad therefore, gave no second thought to disregarding the suggestion to stop and instead referenced the large, clear glass A&W Root Beer jug sitting on the floorboard behind his seat and at my feet. The jug had been filled with tap water from our kitchen sink only days before but already exhibited a green moss floating inside near the bottom. Dad, however, paid this exhibition little or no mind, seeing this provision as being two-fold in its purpose. Number one; abstaining from water encounters during the course of traveling could greatly reduce the possibility of contracting diarrhea. Number two; soft drinks were a waste of money. There was absolutely no reason in the world to stop and by soda water when there was a perfectly good jug of tap water right back there in the floorboard. Never mind that the jug had been with us since we left California and that the green moss seemed to be included in nearly every sip you tried to take. Dad was firmly convinced that the water was still good, because it had originated from our kitchen faucet. Despite our attempts at a subtle rebuttal and our reference to the green hairy growth, Dad's argument always prevailed.

"I don't see anything wrong with that water. That's good California tap water right out of our kitchen faucet," Dad said in a matter of fact tenor. Dad then went into a five-minute discourse about how often he had taken that jug to his work site while working for Granite Construction. He further went on to explain that if that jug of water was good enough for him to take to work, then it was good enough for us to drink out of now! "A little moss in the bottom of the water won't hurt anyone," Dad said with all the confidence of a medical doctor. Dad concluded his statement in a stern voice, saying, "I won't hear another word about it."

That was it, then. We thought the judge had ruled, and there was absolutely nothing that we could do about it. Of course, we still had the heat, the burning bubbled plastic seat covers and Kenny still had his feet on my side of the car. I finally decided to call a truce.

Looking back now, I realize just how calm Kenny truly was during the whole confrontation. As a matter of fact, it was my big brother that turned the hardships of the time into a sweet memory for me. Oh, I'm not saying that everything was suddenly different. The car was just as hot and the seats were just as blistering and his feet were just as intrusive as before, however, after all was said and done, Kenny did something that helped to turn the battlefield into a playground. Once Mom and Dad were again engaged in another deep conversation about some other relatives, Kenny gently reached over and picked up the water jug from beneath my feet and held it up a couple of feet behind Dad's seat. He looked up at me from his bent over position and said quietly with both his eyes bugged out and his two eyebrows lifted,

"How about a drink of some good California moss water? It'll make everything all right!"

We laughed on and off about it for hours. Kenny never was the kind of brother that took pleasure in hurting me or seeing me suffer. God knows, as we got older and made friends, I had plenty of them who had big brothers who seemed to take great delight in causing their siblings pain or embarrassment. Not Kenny. He always seemed to be aware that I was younger and that I was much smaller than he was. For this reason, even during the course of any personal conflicts between us while growing up, he would somehow manage to take my weaknesses into consideration. Kenny never was much of a confrontationalist when it came to being wronged, hurt or mistreated. Passivity was usually the method he selected to handle his problems. Usually, Kenny only became angry or mildly defensive through consistent provocation. He preferred to simply walk away.

On the other hand, I was quite the opposite. I was usually quick to react to any circumstance and also frequently vocal with my opinion. Kenny knew this all too well. Like the time we were both playing in the yard, one warm summer afternoon. We were living then in Los Lomas, California. It was about 1966. I was about to turn ten and Kenny was nearly thirteen. Kenny always seemed more mature for his age than many of his friends, and I can still remember that I often put both his maturity and his passivity to the test.

It had rained the day before. Conditions were perfect to make dirt roads and play Tonka trucks in the side yard of our house at 260 Los Lomas Drive. The small pieces of flat wood we used to scrap out the roads would face little hindrance with the still slightly damp ground. Kenny and I had already spent an hour or so carving the dirt pathways out for our large trucks to use as streets. We had tied strings onto the front of the oversized metal vehicles and we pulled them along behind as we attempted to maneuver them along the created paths. We found this method of moving the toys in the desired directions most effective. It seemed to allow us the pleasure of accomplishing our mission without getting dirt or mud on our clothes. It also saved on wear and tear of the Levi blue jeans our parents found so expensive to replace.

We had no sooner completed the paths and tied the strings to the trucks when Kenny's friend Dennis Brown came streaking down and around Suicide Hill on his ten speed bike. Everyone called the hill Steep Decline Suicide Hill because of the extremely sharp curve at the bottom of what must have been nearly a six-percent grade. Dennis took the curve at a rather high speed and was screaming like a banshee.

Dennis was a curly redheaded freckled-faced boy, who lived at the top of Suicide Hill overlooking the little Los Lomas valley. Poor Dennis often had to exercise his easy-going disposition when our older brother Ronny came around. If Ronny was home and spotted Dennis outside, he would run out of the house shouting to Dennis that he needed to check Dennis' hair for lice. When he caught him, Dennis was usually still straddled across his bicycle seat and Ronny would start picking apart the various strands of Dennis' kinky locks as though he were making a diligent inspection for health reasons. Dennis hated to see Ronny coming and usually immediately asked Kenny or me if Ronny was around. If Ronny was home, Dennis never stayed to chat for very long.

As Dennis made his way down the hill at a break-neck speed, Kenny caught the action through his peripheral vision and dropped the pull string in his hand so quickly that I thought a bee had stung him! Kenny, always being an individual that was easily embarrassed whenever he felt he might be in a position to look foolish, suddenly placed both his hands in his back pockets and began to whistle ever so loudly. As Dennis rapidly approached the scene, Kenny remained in a casual, observant posture. He was obviously pretending for Dennis' sake that he was only an on-looker and not a participant. Kenny had always been rather easily distracted. Even board games or television programs we were enjoying together were often ended abruptly, due to his boredom.

I was immediately angry at both his desire to quit and his embarrassment over Dennis' presence. I knew that once Dennis had departed, the fun would not continue. We had spent a long and tedious time preparing those mud tracks, and now the pleasure was spoiled. Kenny apparently felt he was too old to be playing in the dirt with Tonka trucks. The only possible stance he could take in order to save face upon Dennis' untimely arrival, was that of a mere spectator. I, on the other hand, was not about to let him get by with this. It had taken a very long time to prepare the dirt for play. "Hey man, what's going on?" Dennis shouted at Kenny, while inching his bike a little closer to the picket fence that bordered our front yard.

I did not wait for Kenny's reply. Instead I set out to quickly uncover this charade. I knew that I had the ability to expose this phony for who he truly was, and I deemed it necessary to begin the process in front of the present company. If Kenny was so afraid of embarrassment, then embarrassment was exactly what I would give him. I was mad. How dare him act like he was not involved and was only watching me play in the dirt? Fury continued to rise inside of me. He was the primary instigator, I thought, and it was high time that his precious Dennis knew it!

"Hey man," I screamed at Kenny in a defiant tone. "You said we were going to play with our trucks, now get back here and keep your promise." That will do it I thought.

Instead, in an obvious reaction to the humiliation of the moment, Kenny responded back in a rather nervous sounding voice, "I was never really going to play trucks with you. I was just leading you on so you wouldn't cry. I'm too old for that sorta stuff anyhow." The smirk he was now sporting made me even angrier.

All at once I blurted out, "You're a liar!"

Fully aware that Dennis was well within earshot of his comments, Kenny quickly fired back at me with, "You're a nut, too!"

And that's when I decided to turn the front yard of 260 Las Lomas Drive into a bullring. Like any angry bull that had been taunted and tormented by some arrogant matador, I charged straight at him. "All liars go to hell!" I screamed while making a mad dash for his midsection. As I rushed towards him, my hands swung wildly and I desperately attempted to kick him at the same time. For years my dad had called me The Tasmanian Devil. He would later shorten it to just "Taz." According to Daddy, this cartoon character produced by Warner Brothers best suited my temperament. Daddy had often remarked to my mom how The Taz would be willing to fight a buzz saw.

Kenny on the other hand, had always been more of a non-confrontational kind of person. To him, it was always better to walk away. I would come to discover in later years that non-confrontational people are not cowardly by any means. Most of the time, such individuals often have a strong fear of their own tempers getting out of control. Kenny could be incredibly vicious when provoked for long periods of time. However, he preferred to be the peacemaker. He also was fully aware of the fact that he was not allowed to pick on his little brother, a fact that I was all too well versed in. Kenny, no doubt, felt helpless to defend himself outside of using words.

Now if you are wondering to yourself if I was some kind of a brat, let me help to remove all doubt. I was indeed a brat. I often heard my mother sternly correct Kenny when he became even the slightest bit rough playing with me. "Now Kenny, you be easy with him. He's a lot littler than you and you could hurt him bad," Mom would firmly caution. Now you can certainly rest assured that I took full advantage of that precautionary warning. Even as I attacked Kenny, I knew that Mom had afforded me the upper hand. Looking back now, I realize just how blessed I was to have a big brother who didn't decide to pulverize me and then tell Mom I fell down and hurt myself. Kenny could have easily busted my nose or something and then threaten to kill me if I told Mom that it was anything other than an accident. Instead, Kenny had a great sense of humor. When I came running at him like an African lion defending its kill, he burst into unrestrained laughter. Every time I swung at him, he would push me back by my forehead. It was no doubt, a little bit like watching the three stooges in one of their many comedic skits. The more he deflected my advances, the more outraged I became. And, the more determined I became to give him a piece of my mind, the harder he laughed.

It wasn't fair. His arms were way too long and, of course, everything had to be fair in my book. Once again, I chose to bring out my secret weapon, however inadvertently I may have done so. "No fair hoping you'll win!" I shouted out in a hoarse tone.

"Guess what," Kenny announced. "I am hoping I'll win!"

"Ahhhh..." The scream rose from deep within my chest as I rushed him for the second time flailing my arms in multiple directions. Kenny backed up in an ever-widening circle attempting to prevent my aggression. But I continued my relentless pursuit of vengeance.

Suddenly, Kenny tripped and fell to the ground. I wasted no time taking advantage of the situation. Kenny laughed even more intensely, even after hitting the ground and finding a heap of little brother squarely on top of him. The harder Kenny chuckled, the weaker he became. Kenny's vulnerability made me feel strong, but his annoying laughter made me feel insignificant and non-threatening at best. Kenny held his limp hands up before his face, much like the hands of a weary boxer who had fought fifteen rounds in the ring. Eventually, when his laughter drained him of all remaining strength to hold his hands up, Kenny placed his fingers and palms over his face and just let me pound away. It wasn't as though I was actually making any real headway, you see. Although his hands just partially protected his face, his head wouldn't stop moving from side to side so I could get a clear shot at him. A couple of times, I actually smashed my fist into the ground as I attempted to smack him a good one on the jaw. Kenny was laughing so hard by this time, he had literally started to cough and choke. I had never felt more helpless or insulted in all my short life. After all, Kenny's reaction to my attack made me look like a joke in the eyes of Dennis.

It was then, in a desperate attempt to show the grave seriousness of the onslaught that I reached for a piece of red brick lying only a couple of feet away from his head. As I strained to grasp the fragment where it lay pressed against the weatherworn picket fence, Kenny wiggled free from under my weight. In a moment, he was on his feet again, where he sarcastically proclaimed in a loud voice, "Looks like I'm winning!" He then turned abruptly and ran towards the rear of the house as fast as he could go.

By this time, I had managed to pick up the broken brick and come to a complete upright position. Next, I started chasing after him in an almost animalistic manner, screaming and growling like some she-bear protecting her cubs. What really perturbed me was that his stride was just too long for my little legs. I knew in a flash that I would never be able to catch up.

What followed next can only be described as pure thoughtlessness. My rage quickly got the best of me as I felt the hard substance in my hand and I saw Kenny getting further away with every second. Without giving it a second thought, I reared back and let go of the brick in Kenny's direction. I threw that little jagged piece as hard as I possibly could right at his head. "I'll bring this Goliath down," I thought as I felt the stone leaving my fingers. Strangely enough, at that very moment Kenny was nearing the back left corner of the house where he would have been well within a margin of safety, but he suddenly stopped dead in his tracks and looked back to see if I was still chasing him. It was then that the hurling missile whizzed passed his right ear with only an inch or so to spare. When Kenny heard the "swoosh" of its passing, his eyes bugged out as large as saucers. The expression on his face was one of both bewilderment and fear. Almost as quickly as his initial expression arose, it dissipated into a look of anger, and he lifted a mocking finger in my direction and yelled, "You couldn't hit the broad side of a barn if it was right next to you!"

Instantly, I scanned the fence line for another piece of broken brick. All at once, I spotted a golf ball size rock about midway between me and where Kenny was still standing. No sooner had I spotted the circular stone than his eyes locked in on it as well. Instinctively, he realized where I was headed, and he took off running again around the backside of the house. Like an old west pony express rider attempting to leap from one horse to the other without breaking stride, I made a daring effort to swoop down and gather up the object without losing my momentum. No doubt the mail would have never been delivered if I had been in the saddle. Instead of picking up the rock in one smooth motion while continuing my fast pace, I stumbled and fell on both hands. I got up and tried again but this time I stumbled and fell on my face.

By the time I finally got to my feet and ran to the other side of the house, Kenny was already mounting his three-speed bicycle and heading down the driveway, where he soon met up with his curly haired side-kick and sped away. All I could do was stand there and pant.

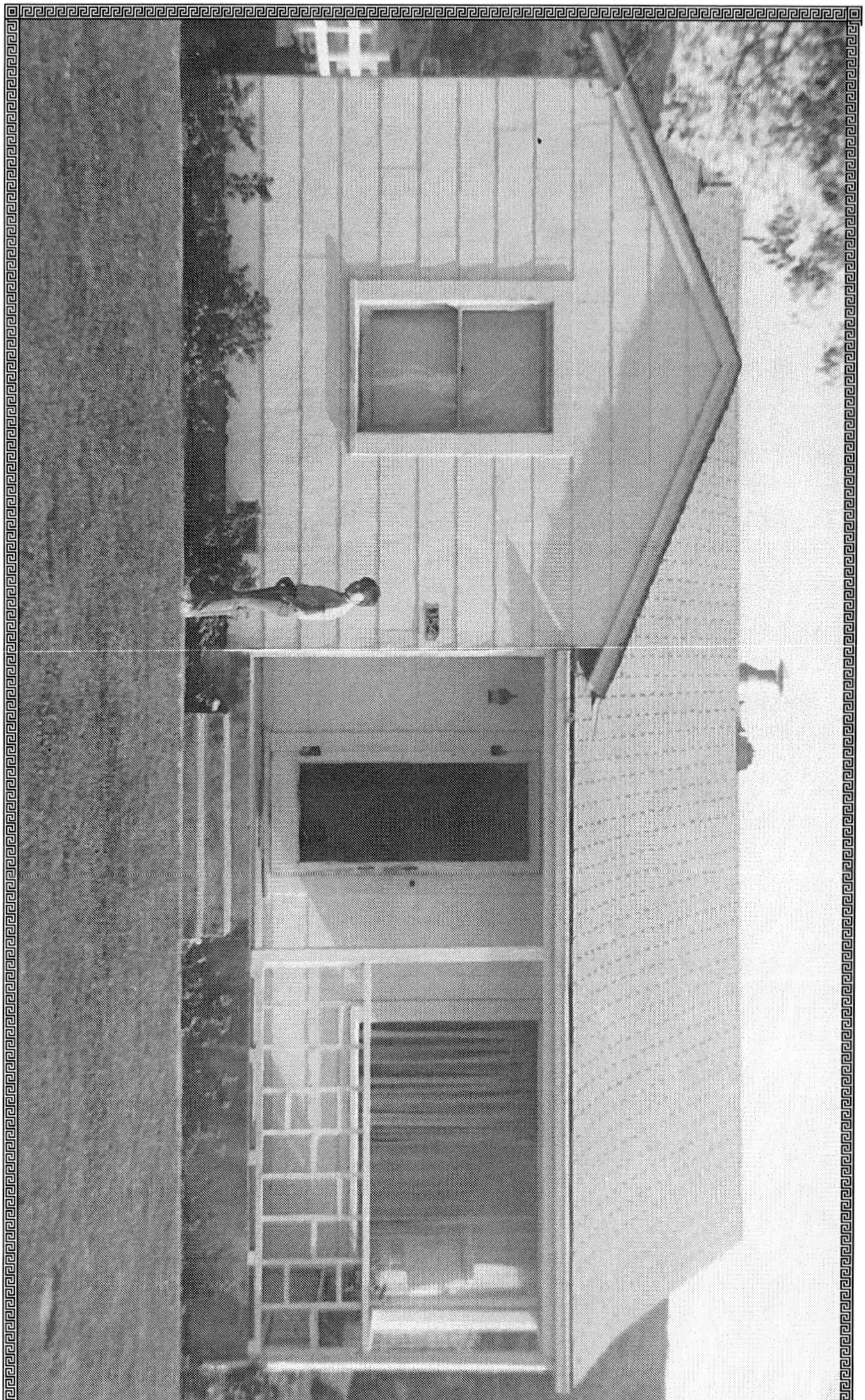

# CHAPTER TWO

## I SEE THE DEVIL

Shortly after the little incident at 260 Las Lomas Drive, we moved to 354 Berry Road. Now this house was still in the same rural community, however, it was clear on the opposite side of the little town. I knew that I would ultimately have to make some new friends after moving into the new venue. I took solace in the fact that Kenny would have to make new friends as well and, for a short time at least he would have to hang close to me.

By this time, Kenny had reached an age where Calvin, Harold and Ronny were beginning to take an interest in him with regard to recreational activities. When one of them took a short jaunt across town for the simple pleasure of getting a coke someplace, Kenny was more and more frequently invited. I, on the other hand, seemed to be another matter altogether. With the three-year difference between our ages, I was no doubt still viewed as more of a babysitting job than a companion.

On one such occasion, I remember one of my brothers asking Kenny if he would like to accompany him to a neighboring town on an errand he had to run. I had looked forward to riding bikes with Kenny up and down the road that led down to Hobo Jungle. It was always a special event to be able to ride down to the end of the single lane paved road where it curved to the left and changed to a dirt lane that wound up through the country side. At that curve in the road

# I SEE THE DEVIL

Kenny and I would take a hard right turn into the thick underbrush. Here there were several large willow trees and a dirt bike trail that led out to the largest willow of all. We often rested for a while under this massive willow. Sitting under the long, dense vine-like branches, we realized we were smack dab in the middle of Hobo Jungle. We called it Hobo Jungle because it was thick with botanical life, and because on more than one occasion, we found the remains of a burnt out campfire.

  This was a place where no doubt some hobos had found shelter from the cold and damp weather often associated with that region during the winter months. We loved sitting beneath the green canopy of the old willow. I always craved adventure and it was somewhat of a thrill for me to think about who or what we might ride in upon as we passed through the vinery curtain. Yet, it was still just a little too frightening for someone of my young age to attempt to ride down there alone. Without my older brother, I would never even dream of venturing into such a dangerous environment. I knew regardless of what peril might lie there that Kenny was big enough and strong enough to protect us. I was what younger brothers are supposed to be, weak and defenseless.

  You can only imagine how disappointed I was one day when Kenny was offered the opportunity to leave with Harold. Sure, he would have a lot of fun, but what was I supposed to do in the meantime? You can rest assured about one thing: Hobo Jungle was off my agenda for the day. I guess I must have made my disappointment rather apparent to Kenny. I'm sure my bottom lip was nearly dragging the ground as Kenny turned to observe my reaction to Harold's invitation. It wasn't that I was attempting in any way to appear more saddened than I truly was. The reality of it is I have never been very good at hiding my feelings. Kenny was quick to pick up a clear reading on my face and therefore found no difficulty in determining my emotions.

Then Kenny did something that totally amazed me at the time. He turned around to my older brother Harold and snarled his nose, shook his head back and forth from side to side and said, " Nah... I don't think so this time but thanks anyhow! I think I'll just hang out here with Larry. We're fixin' to head down to Hobo Jungle or something."

"Come on man, come with me," Harold urged even more emphatically now, in hopes of persuading Kenny to change his mind.

"No, really! It's all right," Kenny replied casually. "I'll go with you next time for sure."

"Okay, have it your way," Harold replied appearing a tiny bit frustrated as he opened the car door of his old Mercury and stepped inside.

As our sibling slowly drove around the last corner that led from our street to the main highway, Kenny placed his right hand on my left shoulder and asked, "So, what do you want to do?" Still stunned by his unexpected reaction and just thankful to be doing anything at all with him that day, I completely forgot all about Hobo Jungle for the moment.

I looked at him in a rather bewildered manner and replied softly, "I don't know, what do you want to do?" With a pondering expression on his face, much like someone baffled by a difficult puzzle, he stared at the ground.

All at once he jerked up his head and cocked it to one side, lifting both eyebrows simultaneously as if he had been surprised by something. "I know," he said excitedly. "Let's play 'I see the Devil!'" I found myself gazing at him for a fairly long time before finally responding to his statement.

"I see the Devil?" I questioned him like someone not sure if they were hearing correctly. "What in the world is 'I see the Devil' anyway?" My confusion as to what he was suggesting was becoming even more apparent by the second. Now before you can understand why I was questioning Kenny's choice of games and before you can truly comprehend the statement I was about to make, you must realize that the subject of the devil to us was never a good one. I suppose that there may be those who could find the very concept of playing such a game rather offensive to their Christian scruples. However, keep in mind that it was a much more naïve world in the 1960s than it is today. Christians still permitted their children to participate in Halloween, even having spook houses in the church to help raise funds. All the while, those same church leaders could be found preaching against such things as TV and sport events. Christians told ghost stories to one another in those days and then spoke out against playing pool.

I couldn't imagine for the life of me why Kenny would even think of such a thing. Now let me further say, before you become convinced that I might be talking about one of the so called "Saints" that attended my daddy's church. Keep in mind that we were raised old line Pentecost, part of what was known as "Full Gospel Christians" or "Holy Rollers." I had often witnessed individuals in Pentecostal services who appeared to be devil possessed. We were taught that the scriptures bore witness of such individuals, and we had seen them with our own eyes. Sometimes they jerked and even frothed at the mouth. There had even been some occasions when it sounded like someone else speaking out of the person, other than the one being exorcised.

At the little storefront church where my daddy pastored, we encountered someone like that nearly every Sunday. This of course is not the kind of subject matter you would expect to find in the song my brother Ronny would later write about the little meeting place. In addition to all the wonderful services and great preaching that transpired in that little storefront, there were also quite a few confrontations with the devil. There were bars and nightclubs all around the little converted bathhouse where my dad pastored in Pajaro. Often, the drunks would stagger into a service only to find themselves at an altar of prayer with a number of saints gathered around them praying for the devil to come out. Sometimes hobos would be nearly dragged into service by a couple of women in our church who loved to lead the old drunks to salvation. Bums, winos and other bathless vagabonds could be found in abundance just a block away.

This was where the original Hobo Jungle existed, that lay directly below the bridge that separated Pajaro from Watsonville. This was also the place from where we borrowed the name for our little hideaway under the willow tree. Usually when we got to church on Sunday morning, while my dad was lifting the drunks up off the front steps, Kenny and I picked up the red mountain wine bottles and the Ripple bottles scattered along the curbside where parishioners would soon be parking. We also had the gross task of removing the filthy containers from the grassy enclosure that ran the full length of the building. The look of wine bottles dotting the landscape always seemed to create an eyesore for those attending our little meetinghouse. Winos seemed to walk that street at every hour of the day. Kenny and I had become so accustomed to bums asking for a dime or quarter that we started asking them for change, before they had a chance to ask us. They would almost always reply the same way to our question, "I wazzz ganna ask you the sameee thing."

Those kinds of people made me think of the devil and when Kenny suggested the game, I immediately thought he was suggesting either we act drunk or possessed. "I don't want to play like we're at church!" I suddenly protested with a soured expression, as though I had just tasted something rancid.

"Not church!" Kenny fired back in a frustrated tone. "Where did you ever get the idea that I wanted to play church?"

"Well," I replied defensively, "that's where you see the devil."

"No, man," Kenny waved his hand before his chest, while shaking his head in disagreement at the same time. "I'm talking about a real game."

# I SEE THE DEVIL

"A game?" I asked displaying an obvious air of disbelief. "What kind of a game is 'I see the Devil' anyway?" Kenny just shrugged his shoulders and raised his eyebrows.

"I don't know," he replied, openly displaying his frustration at my lack of imagination. "Why can't we just make it up as we go?"

"Well, how do we start?" I asked.

"No big deal," Kenny went on to explain, as he lifted the palms of his hands in my direction. "We just wing it."

"Oh, this ain't gonna be any fun," I said with a smirk on my lips.

"I bet it will!" Kenny said, leaning in near to my face and opening his eyes wide. "And I bet you get scared in the meantime, too." Now Kenny seemed to be smirking.

"So you're gonna try to scare me?" I questioned.

"Nah..." Kenny said, ever so confident. "We're gonna try to get scared together at the same time."

"But it's broad daylight" I protested. "How do you get scared in the daytime? I mean, I could see getting scared at night, but when the sun's still up?"

Kenny held up his index finger, winked at me and slowly spoke. "Watch!" Then using a mysterious voice, perhaps borrowed from some Boris Karloff movie, he motioned for me to come with him and said, "Follow me."

The two of us slowly crept around the front left-hand corner of the house. We went past our mom's Easter lilies, which we had often imagined as swash bucking pirates attempting to steal our large bounty of treasure. These poor pitiful souls had often became decapitated for their fruitless efforts. Kenny and I had many sword fights with them. However, at that time, they were actually recovering quite well due to the fact that Mom had forbidden any further contact with the pirates of "Lilly Island." At the present time, our little adventure would lead us past the blooming pedestals and closer to the white split railed fence that bordered our property.

Kenny had taken on a cloak and dagger attitude about this strange game and I had to admit to myself that he was making things quite interesting. Just as we reached the far corner at the back of our house, Kenny reached behind him. Without looking, he put his right hand on my chest and said, "Stop!" The abrupt manner in which he brought our little trek to a halt, immediately caused my heart to start racing. I have often wondered if at that moment he could feel my heart pounding wildly within me. Perhaps his hand was placed strategically on my chest in order to feel my heart beat. And yet, he was definitely right about his previous prediction. We had scarcely begun our daylight journey and I was already getting scared!

Suddenly without warning, Kenny snapped. "There, do you see it?" With his arm outstretched and his finger pointed straight as an arrow, he tried to focus my attention on something that had moved over by the old shed, directly located behind our weather beaten garage and to the right of the cornrows planted by our dad. Kenny and I had been raised up in church all of our lives and we were fully aware that there were certainly two sides to every story told in the Bible. If there was a David, then there was also a Goliath. If there was a Job, then there was also a devil. Now as far as I was concerned, it was one thing to read about giants and demons, it was quite another to have to confront one in person. Especially when there was no dad or mom close around to run to for assistance. I really didn't relish the idea of being either David or Job at this point in my life. As far I was concerned, I was still dependent on others older and more experienced than I was.

This for Kenny and I, would in fact, become a lifelong lesson about entertaining the right spirit. We came to realize very quickly that day that if you go looking for the devil, you are very likely to find him. One must be careful in the quest for knowledge and truth. Anytime you expect the devil to interfere with your life through situations and circumstances you can rest assured he won't disappoint you. If on the other hand, you expect God to intervene in your behalf, he will never let you down!

Unfortunately, Kenny and I were not seasoned enough in scriptural knowledge at the time, to realize this valuable tidbit of information. We fully expected to see the evil one. After all, we initially set out to find the devil and it hadn't taken us very long to accomplish our mission. "Stay here," Kenny said quickly. "Don't move from this position," he ordered. "I'll be back in a few seconds." His voice was barely above a whisper now. Slowly, Kenny tiptoed around the corner of the house and pressed his back against its shingled outer wall. Within just a few moments, he had inched his way up to the back steps leading inside our home and completely out of my field of vision.

For the next few moments, I felt as though Kenny had been gone forever. I saw nothing nor heard even the slightest sound coming from his direction. I half expected to peek around the corner and discover some gargoyle type creature munching on his remains. Fear, however, gave way to suspicion and then I began to wonder if this was some kind of a double cross. Perhaps he would attempt to circle around the house and sneak up behind me. After all, he had a promise to keep about getting me scared. I might be able to deny the racing heartbeat he discovered earlier under my white t-shirt, but there would be no denying a pair of running feet if he should he manage to get the drop on me.

Not really eager to take my eyes off the old shed, yet reluctant to allow myself to fall victim to a trick, I glanced over my right shoulder towards the breeze swept pirates of Lily Island. I half expected that at any minute a pair of peeking eyes would cast a sneaky gaze in my direction from that far front corner of our dwelling. Like a lion in the wild, Kenny would no doubt remain poised for the right moment to pounce. However, I would make certain through my keen senses and sharp eyesight that the beast would not be successful in stalking his prey this time!

Instead, what happened next turned my blood to ice water. Kenny let out a blood-curdling scream from somewhere on the other side of the house. I felt my body inadvertently jerk the very second the shrill outcry broke the silence. I stood deathly still for a moment or two pondering what I should do. Perhaps my greatest fears had come true and, in fact, some scaley creature from the underworld had really decided to make Kenny an afternoon snack. Or, I thought as a wave of calmness swept over my body for a moment, this could simply be a small part of a bigger plan. Kenny could just be setting the stage for a much larger roll to follow. The only thing that still bothered me about the whole situation was that the scream sounded like genuine horror. It certainly didn't seem scripted, if you know what I mean. It didn't feel like an act put on to convince the audience of the performance. No, this was the real McCoy all right.

Suddenly, like an ambulance running code three and streaking past with its blaring siren alerting all present to clear the path for its passage, Kenny came rushing around the back corner of the house yelling at the top of his lungs! "Ahhhh…" The tone of his voice sounded lower than before and somewhat hoarse, like it was bellowing out from the depths of his stomach. In the process, he nearly trampled right over me. I had never seen such a look of terror on anyone's face in all my life. His eyes were as big as silver dollars and he never stopped screeching until he ran all the way past Lilly Island and on to the front lawn! I stood there watching him in total disbelief. Like someone completely transfixed on a winning racehorse crossing over the finish line, I just stayed there looking at him from a distance as he attempted to catch his breath.

All at once it occurred to me, whatever it was he was fleeing from in the back yard might very well be standing behind me right now! Without ever looking around to verify my suspicions, I let out with my own version of a horror flick scream and took off running as fast as my two tiny legs could carry me. I made a beeline directly for Kenny. I just knew in

# I SEE THE DEVIL

my heart though, if I tripped and fell now some bug eyed, pointed eared demon with poison dripping fangs and sharp curving claws, would swoop down and scoop me up for his dinner! "Come on legs," I thought. "Don't fail me now!" Kenny was all the way up to the edge of the grass that bordered the road by this point in time. He was standing sideways with one foot on the paved street and the other still on the lawn. I had to reach him somehow, I thought. I had to get to him before the monster got to me.

Kenny would manage someway to protect me once I got to him, I said to myself. However, Kenny wouldn't even see me get eaten if the creature caught me I finally decided. He wasn't even looking in my direction.

Kenny was still struggling to get air back into his lungs and was bent over at the waist, with his face pointed towards the ground and his hands resting on his knees. I didn't have to look behind me to verify exactly what was chasing me. I already knew that the fiendish pursuer was in fact he whom we had come looking for in the first place. It was none other than the devil himself, I thought. I wasn't even a bit surprised when I discovered that the devil had already vanished into thin air once I had reached the safety of Kenny's presence. After all, I knew just how clever he was about cloaking his presence through the means of a supernatural disappearing act. But I wasn't stupid enough to think he was no longer there, either. I had heard the song in Children's Church that went:

> The devil is a sly ole fox,
> if I had my way I'd put him a in a box.
> I'd put him in a box and throw away the key,
> for all the mean tricks he's played on me.

So then, the devil was a trickster. He was an illusionist, a magician. He could make you believe whatever he needed you to believe for the moment. He was there all right. I knew he was there, we just couldn't see him. That meant he had the ability to reach out from nowhere at any given time and pluck us from the land of the living. I was pretty much trained to accept the fact that the god of this world had free reign with regard to whatever he chose to do to you in this present life. I also knew that he had no authority over your being once you finally made it home to heaven. However, given the current situation, the latter was of very little comfort.

Oh, if I only knew then what I know now: how truly victorious one can be in Christ! I didn't realize then that it was a matter of attitude and the word of God in my mouth. Nonetheless, I had the right attitude for attracting the wrong spirit and the perfect fear to generate an imperfect afternoon. Now I realize that one can choose to simply explain away the whole matter as just immature imagination. Or, one can come to understand that the entire ordeal was more than likely a result of true demonic activity preying upon two kids with little spiritual experience.

"Are you all right?" Kenny spoke now in a hoarse breathy tone, still trying to fill his heaving lungs with some much-needed oxygen.

"Yeah, I'm okay," I said, panting rapidly between each word.

With his usually well groomed hair now wind blown and his face bright red from the sudden burst of exercise, Kenny looked up at me with his hands still resting on his locked knees and said something that gave me horrible dreams that night. "Larry, I promise you man, and I'm not kidding. Larry, I saw him!" Kenny's eyes seemed even larger than before, as he informed me of his recent and unfortunate encounter.

"Saw who?" I quickly responded, feeling my heart rate increasing again.

"I saw the devil." No doubt, my eyes became as big as the headlights on my dad's fifty-seven Chrysler Imperial.

"Where?" I quietly questioned. Kenny's expression swiftly changed from appearing horrified to utter bewilderment. He lifted his head slowly and lowered his eyes to the ground simultaneously. He looked like he had just discovered that the lawn was missing.

"Back there," he muttered softly, while pointing his raised left thumb slightly outward, in the direction from which he had bolted only minutes ago.

"Where back there?" I asked with a trembling voice.

"In the old tool shed," Kenny said the words quickly and then swallowed hard. "No joke, Larry. He's in there!" I had never heard of anything more bazaar in all my life and yet I truly believed it with all my heart. After all, Kenny wouldn't lie about a thing like this I thought. Or maybe he would.

"Kenny, if you're making this up man, I'm gonna kill you!"

"No, man, I wouldn't do something like that! This is for real." Kenny stood his full stature now as he walked closer to where I was standing and placed his hands on his hips. There was a long pause in the conversation between us before he finally broke the silence with a question. "What do you think we ought to do?" Kenny didn't wait for a reply before continuing with a statement. "I mean we can't tell Mom, she'll never believe us."

"Yeah, but maybe she might not make us come back outside if she knew about it," I blurted.

"Yeah, and we're gonna look pretty stupid too, if there's no devil back there after Dad gets home and investigates." Kenny emphasized his comments by rolling his eyes. "We're going to have to check this out further," Kenny now announced, while gesturing to me to follow him.

"You've got to be crazy!" I shouted out. "There ain't no way I'm going back there to find the devil." I was starting to sweat profusely now, the thought of actually seeing ole cloven hoofs wasn't exactly on my wish list. This was a bad idea, I thought. I'm not going to make matters worse by playing right into the devil's hands.

"You coming, or not?" Kenny was already standing at the right front corner of our house.

"This is nuts!" I said with a sarcastic tone to my voice, while making my way in Kenny's direction.

"Come on man, I'll prove to you that I'm not lyin'."

Great! Just what I needed, I thought. Proof that he wasn't lying. Kenny began to explain what initially happened as we slowly made our way towards the paint bare garage directly in front of the old shed. Kenny started speaking at a low volume in order to keep Satan from hearing us approach, I supposed. "At first, I went over there behind the garage so that I could find a place to hide. I was gonna call you over and jump out and scare you. When I was looking around for a place to get out of sight, I thought about hiding in the old shed for a minute and then making noises through the open window." Kenny's voice began to waiver a little and his eyes started to water. I knew by his physical reaction to the story he was telling, he couldn't possibly be making it all up. Kenny went on even softer now, as we got closer to the front of the garage. "When I looked into the old shed's window, Larry I promise you, I saw him looking right back at me." Kenny was really starting to perspire heavily now. Although it was a warm sunny day I could tell that he was not actually sweating because of the heat. Even though I was only ten years old, I could tell the difference between a good performance and the real deal. As far as I was concerned, it didn't get any more real than this. The more convinced I became that Kenny was genuinely shaken up, the more frightened I became. However, regardless of how scared I really was for the moment at the thought of running head long into the lord of the underworld, I still was unable to resist the drawing power of Kenny's persuasive manner.

Once again, Kenny leaned over towards me and cupped his hand over my left ear. "Follow me," he said in a shaky voice. "We'll sneak around the right side of the garage. He probably won't be expecting us to come up from that direction. From there you'll be able to get a clear view of him." Kenny now seemed to strategize with all the confidence of an experienced military commander. "Just maybe," Kenny went on, "we'll be able to see him before he sees us." To a ten-year-old kid, it sounded like a well thought-out plan. After all, Kenny had been our combat leader on all those previous missions in Aromas, why not trust his judgment now? So, I literally followed in his every footstep to the right side of the garage. Now I will admit that right about this time, I sincerely hoped that this particular incident would be virtually uneventful. I would in fact, be willing to settle for an unexplained sighting, one that could be chalked up to mere imagination. However, I must also admit that Kenny's prior encounter had been all too real to simply ignore. Yet, there was one other thing to consider in the course of our investigation.

You see Daddy had not always been the pastor to the little storefront church. One of the former pastors was ole Brother Kelsey. Now, Sister Kelsey still attended the church, though it had been quite sometime since her husband had passed away. And, on certain occasions, she found herself reminiscent of the days when her husband stood on the platform to minister at the little church. I soon came to realize something significant, shortly after this summer afternoon encounter with the devil. Evidently, all that was necessary to scare Kenny half out of his mind, was to mix one part Sister Kelsey's memory of her husband and one part Kenny's extreme fear of ghosts. Perhaps Kenny just wasn't saying at the time that he believed it to be a ghost hanging around the tool barn. I can still recall the event that took place at my daddy's church that involved Sister Kelsey and Brother Kelsey, too, for that matter. It seemed to be the very start of Kenny's belief in disembodied spirits. With its dark dingy walls and brown painted ceiling, its dim, discolored globes of light, suspended from the high flat surface above the heads of the little group on long dangling wires. There its old blackish brown theatre seats sat with much of their wood scarred and splitting. Most of the chairs exposing the blonde, jagged surface beneath their faded paint still brandished their original cold iron frames, which had been bolted to the archaic, lusterless hardwood floors they rested on. The old converted bathhouse from the 1920s still boasted an atmosphere of an old line Pentecostal church from a bygone era.

Yet, it was here, in this almost depressing atmosphere of broken down furnishings and dilapidated walls, that we had some incredibly exciting and old-fashioned camp meeting services! There was, of course those various occasions when something rather strange would take place that would ultimately alter the expected outcome of the meeting.

Like when Sister Kelsey stood up to testify one cold winter's night. She could barely speak when it came her turn during testimony service for wiping the tears and blowing her nose in her handkerchief. "Brother Hinson," Sister Kelsey spoke loudly, "a moment ago, when you were up thare on the platform a talkin' about the Lord, I saw my husband Herman, a standin' up thare just like he use ta, when we was a pastorin' here so long ago. I saw him standin' up thare, just about whare that youngen' of yours is a standin' right now!" Kenny naturally took that to mean that there was in fact the ghost of Herman, standing right next to him. Kenny had been warming his hands at the ancient gas heater that inadequately attempted to provide warmth for the entire auditorium. Upon hearing that Herman was back from the dead and had chosen to stand directly beside him, he let out loudly with a cry for Mama, extending both arms straight out in her direction at the same time. Poor Sister Kelsey didn't even get to finish her testimony for the loud weeping that followed.

It took forever to calm him and even longer to convince him that Sister Kelsey was simply remembering when her husband preached to the small congregation, while standing near the very place where Kenny had been warming himself. Panic stricken from the spooky incident, Kenny's childhood was never to be the same. He was still seeing ghosts well up into his teens. Dad would always attempt to remind Kenny that the devil was simply trying to torment him. Kenny would eventually get a grip on his ghostly fears. However, this time, I wasn't certain if this weren't one of those strange visitations. This rabbit trail down memory lane both comforted me and yet troubled me too.

While Kenny was no doubt certain that he had in fact seen ole slough foot, he may have just as well misunderstood what his eyes had witnessed. After all, he had misinterpreted what Sister Kelsey meant about her husband's appearance. On the other hand, there was no Sister Kelsey to blame for all the confusion. Maybe, I thought, he's become his own confusion. Yet, the thought still nagged at my brain, what if Kenny was right? The very concept of such a thing nearly froze me in my tracks. The one thing that drove me was that Kenny would have gone on without me and I would have been left standing there all alone for easy pickings. I had always heard that there was strength in numbers, so I hurried to catch up.

I regretted my decision almost immediately, once I reached Kenny. There, directly ahead, at a left diagonal angle, stood the old weatherworn shack. Daddy stored his hoes, rakes, shovels, seeds and lawn mower in that shack. There were even a few nails in there as well and there was no telling what the devil could do with all that stuff, I pondered. For some strange reason, the old, slightly leaning, tinned roof structure reminded me more of haunted house than a tool shed. Even though chicken wire stretched the full length of its long glassless window, I thought the grayish colored wooden planks, which made up its walls looked somewhat fitting for a demon to inhabit. Attempting to focus beyond this visual barrier seemed to be a difficult task at best. Not being able to watch the devil watching us, further heighten our tension. We felt entirely at a disadvantage, not to mention completely defenseless. Yet, there we were, standing right out in the open and still in a crouched position. You would have thought we were hiding behind some one-way mirror, completely obstructing Satan's view of us. In reality, we knew that we were the ones unable to see him.

Once again, Kenny turned around and looked at me with wide eyes and a gaping mouth. Then he began to whisper. I had to strain to hear. "Oh, God! Larry, he's probably looking straight at us!" Kenny's wavering voice now left me no conclusion but to believe he was about to lose his cool. This did absolutely no good whatsoever for my personal confidence. As a matter of fact, I nearly soiled my pants. I could feel a weird tremble starting in my knees and working its way up my legs. I wanted to run, however, I really did not know if I could. I realized at this moment we were face to face with the most evil, the most diabolical creature that God ever made anywhere. I fully expected his pitchfork to come flying at us any moment through the wired window. I was already playing out the entire scenario in my head. First it would tear right through the chicken wire and pen one of our shoes strategically to the ground. Furthermore, while the remaining individual ran for help, he would leap out of the old tool shed to claim his victim as his prize. Whichever one of us was caught would never be seen or heard from again. I didn't know what to do and Kenny's eyes were still glued to the window as if he were frozen in time.

All at once, he pointed a shaking finger in the shed's direction and blurted out, "I see him, there he is!" In a moment of shear terror, my eyes darted from Kenny to the window of the ancient barn. I could not believe what I saw. There, on the other side of the chicken wire, from the dark recesses of the broken down shack two large glowing eyes stared back at us! The eyes seemed angry and appeared to be almost mocking our stupidity. The devil was in fact really here, I thought. I tried to say, "Let's run!" but I couldn't find my voice.

Suddenly, the eyes started to move. Yet they never broke their frightening stare at us. First they floated to the right of the window and finally to the left. All the while, they continued to gaze unflinching in our direction. The devil seemed to be pacing back and forth in the shadows of the shed, like some caged lion unable to free himself from its prison. Could it be, I thought for a moment, that the devil is actually captured inside the old shed and can't get out? Surely Daddy wouldn't have trapped him in there without telling Mom and us kids to stay clear of the place. Maybe Daddy had placed him in the shed and had simply forgot to tell anyone during the excitement of going to get some anointing oil or something. Maybe he didn't want to frighten anyone with the news of Satan's presence until he returned home and eliminated the problem. After all, I pondered, he was anointed and would use some anointing oil for just about everything. And of course, who could bind the devil better than my own dad could!

  This was, for me at least, a glimmer of hope in an otherwise very bleak situation. I turned to Kenny and shouted loudly, "Kenny, maybe Daddy locked him in there and he can't get free. You know, Daddy is a great man of God and he probably just used his anointing to put the devil in there." My words flew from my lips at a speed equal to that of bullets firing from the barrel of a sub-machine gun. I'm not even sure if Kenny really understood them. I figured the fallen angel was only there temporarily, while Dad went for some backup in order to help him pray and cast the devil back into hell. Many times Dad called the brethren in the church to help him cast out a demon in someone possessed. Of course, I thought, this was the devil himself, and would no doubt require more than just a few people praying. That would explain why Dad had been gone so long. It takes time to collect that many people to cast out the prince of darkness!

  All at once, Kenny shattered my desperate dream of impending rescue with a hopeless statement that genuinely served to chill me straight to the bone. "Nah..." Kenny said, with an air of confidence in his tone. "Devils can't be confined to a building or anything. They can go anywhere anytime they want to. He's just playing with us."

Each breath I took was coming faster and harder now. My heart was beating ninety miles an hour at the thought that the devil was actually planning the most hideous method he could think of to annihilate us. Without warning, the eyes within the darkened interior seemed to spring forward and down out of our range of sight. "Oh, no!" I thought in a moment of near panic. "Is the devil going down through the ground, only to pop up right beneath our very feet?" Kenny didn't wait to find out the answer to any such questions that were no doubt racing through his mind as well. Neither did I.

All at once Kenny let go with a scream that seemed to come up from the very soles of his shoes. He sounded like one of those air raid sirens utilized in World War II for warning of incoming enemy aircraft. My scream probably sounded more like a little girl's. The two of us somehow found the strength to tear out running at a feverish pace. By the time we finally reached the back door, our attempt to get inside looked like a scene taken directly from the "Keystone Cops." We pushed and shoved each other out of the way. We were tripping, falling down and trying to squeeze past one another through the doorway at the very same time. When we actually did manage to get through the door, we burst into the laundry room like a cork popping out of a bottle. Kenny slammed into the wash machine at the far end of the narrow room, while I went sprawling across the floor. Neither one of us really got hurt, but our slightly less than delicate entrance made such a clatter that it summoned Mom's attention.

I was still in the process of picking myself up from the linoleum surface when mom stepped around the corner from the kitchen to observe where we had crashed. "What are you boys trying to do, tear the house down?" Mom said in a stern voice. "I don't want you wrestling in the house. You're liable to break something. I thought I told you two to stay outside and play. It's a pretty day and you need to get right back outside if you're going to scuffle around." Now, the last thing I wanted to do was to go back outside where the devil was. I was ready to start spilling my guts about what we had seen

# I SEE THE DEVIL

and how we came to see it. Surely if we explained to her that we had encountered the devil she wouldn't make us go back out there! Kenny, on the other hand, must have realized just how far fetched such a story would sound.

When I started trying to share the little incident we had just experienced, he abruptly interrupted my story with a chuckle, placing his right hand on my left shoulder and squeezing. "Mom," Kenny now spoke with a humorous tenor to his tone, while simultaneously shaking his head from side to side. "I was just playing around with Larry. We really didn't see anything. Larry just got scared, that's all."

"You're lying," I blurted out in a loud shout of protest. "We both saw his eyes!" I announced while using my right index finger to point in the direction of the devil's last known location. Kenny started applying even more pressure now to my left collarbone, in order to signal me to shut up.

"Kenny, you stop scaring your brother like that. Somebody could get hurt," Mom firmly demanded.

"I will, Mom." Kenny now stepped into the role of the repentive, yet dutiful and obedient son. "Sorry, Mom. It won't happen again," Kenny quickly reassured her.

"You don't need to be playing like that anyhow," Mom went on continuing her lecture. "The devil's real and you could get him after you."

That's just wonderful, I thought. He's already after us only Kenny won't let me tell you about it. Kenny must be afraid of getting a whipping for causing the devil to come after us in the first place. Yeah, I decided, that would explain everything. No wonder he didn't want mom to know about it. Mom's lack of information as to the devil being trapped in the tool shed would seem to verify my suspicions that Dad hadn't told her about it either.

"Tell me," Mama went on to question with a tinge of curiosity present in her tone, "when you were in the yard playing did either one of you see my cat? I haven't seen her all day." Although Dad had never really cared for animals around the house, Mom's gray striped alley cat seemed to be

52

the one exception to the rule. The cat really was just a stray that had already been living under the house when we first moved in, and actually never belonged to anyone exclusively, including Mama. This adopted feline family member, would often rendezvous with her at the back steps of our house, as Mom would greet her with a saucer of milk. It was there that Mom would speak to and caress her furry friend. Mom had become rather attached to the little creature and went onto explain that she was concerned it might have crawled off someplace to die. "It may have been chewed up by an old mean dog." She went on ranting as her imagination starting getting the best of her. "You know, there's an awful lot them around this neighborhood."

"Nope, I didn't see your cat," I announced with tone of certainty, but Kenny was slow to respond. He appeared to be lost in deep concentration for the moment. He then looked at me and rolled his eyes and a grin broke out instantly from the corners of his mouth. He pressed his lips together and let out a deep sigh through his nostrils. He lifted his left eyebrow ever so slightly, as he peered at Mama from the corner of his left eye.

"Yeah," he said, as a chuckle mingled with the word. "I think I've seen your cat all right."

"You have?" Mom replied in a voice filled with exuberance. "Where?"

"You'll find the dev... I mean the cat, in the old tool shed." Upon Dad's return home, we discovered that the gray alley cat had been playing around Daddy's feet while he was putting something away in the shed. Somehow, Dad had inadvertently closed the door behind him before the cat could manage to get out. From that day forward, whenever Kenny and I saw the appearance of Mom's stray cat, we privately and jokingly, remarked to one another, "I see the devil."

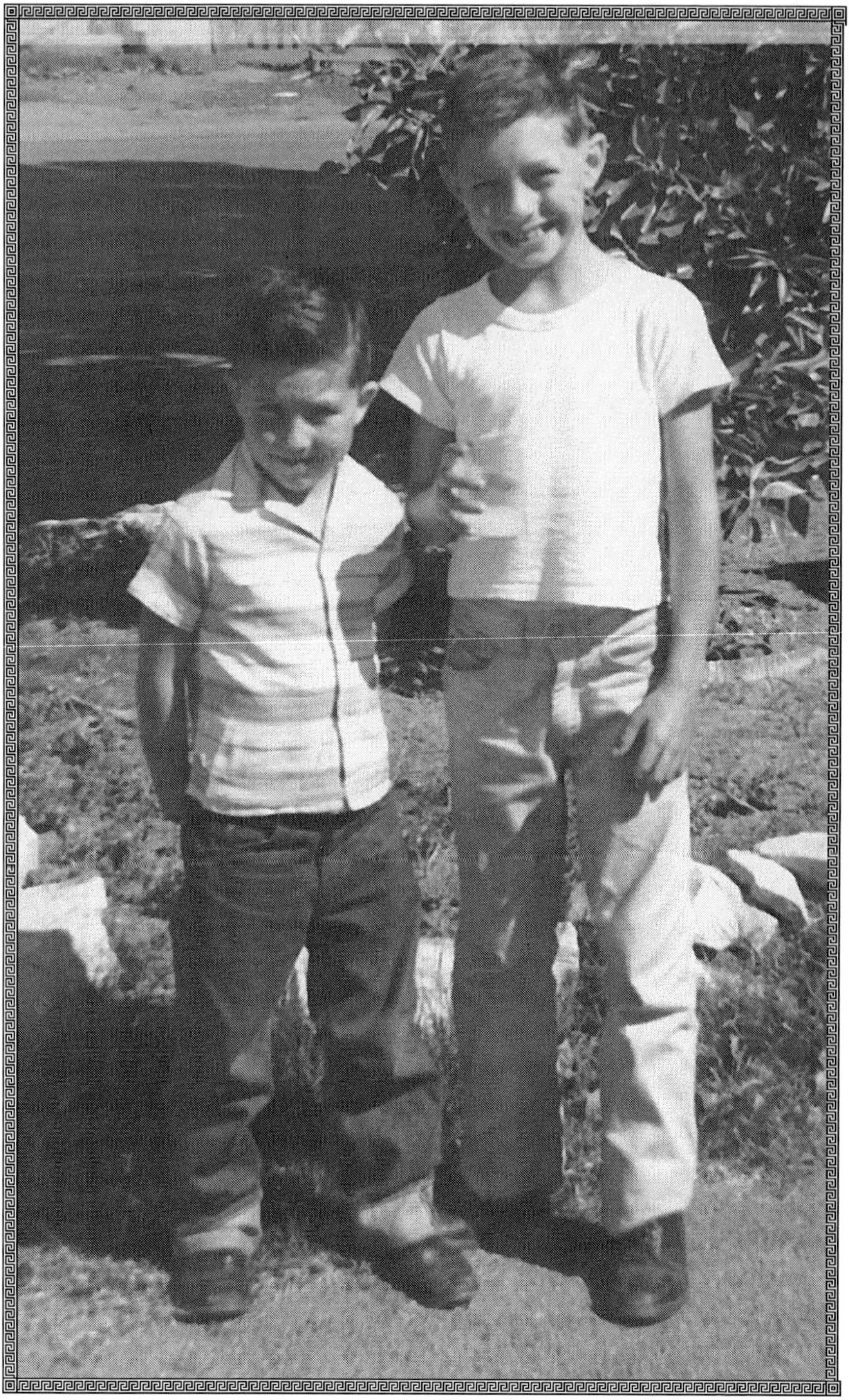

# CHAPTER THREE

# NOW THAT'S ENTERTAINMENT

Being raised in a very strict religious environment, we found ourselves extremely limited when it came to the area of extracurricular activities. Sometimes, just for fun, Kenny and I would play chicken with one another. We would get astride our junk yard specials and ride the bikes nearly head on into one another on the old two lane leading down to Hobo Jungle. That soon came to a stop, however, one Saturday afternoon when our daddy took away our bikes and sold them. He didn't mind our demolition derbies all that much, so long as we were still using our battle scarred scrap heaps to do so. After he purchased brand new bicycles for us, imported from Tennessee, he naturally became outraged when we continued participating in our collision championships. We actually didn't mind all that much that he sold the bikes. By this time we were getting much older anyway, and in fact, felt we had a much larger source of entertainment.

Because of our Pentecostal background, we were automatically prohibited from playing with such vices as dice, all kinds of card games, and billiards. These were often referred to as "Tricks of the Devil" because they could draw you away from God towards gambling. Movie theaters were called "Cesspool Cinemas," and anyone caught in one when the Lord split the eastern sky would go straight to hell in a hand basket. Even sports activities were largely discouraged, due their ability to entice you to live frivolous and flippant lives. Not to mention the fact that they would inevitably keep you out of church.

You see, gambling had long been established as a cardinal sin. Why, way back at the foot of the cross on which Christ was crucified the Roman soldiers gambled for his seamless robe. For this reason alone, there was enough evidence to justify preaching and believing against anything remotely related to spinning the wheel of chance.

In those days, full gospel people were only interested in things directly associated with the rapture of the church. We had already read enough books and heard enough sermons about the subject of the Lord's soon return that we came to believe that the world couldn't possibly wax any worse before His arrival. Television shows like NBC's "Laugh In" fully indicated how wicked and perverse the world had become. Prayer had been taken from our schools in '63 and the Vietnam War was dividing our country right down the middle. We felt that if ever there was a time when the Lord needed to come back for His saints, it was then. For this reason, if you were doing anything other than going to work, school, winning souls for Jesus and attending church every time the doors were opened, you were going to miss the rapture!

With our dad being the pastor of the church we attended, there was absolutely no possibility of missing the advent of the Lord in our house. We were guaranteed shoe-ins, due to our never failing attendance. So if we were to have any form of excitement or enjoyment, it had to come directly from the church itself. It was only natural then that if our entertainment would be coming from the little Brooklyn Street church that our entertainers would be selected from the congregation. However, keep in mind that in order to qualify as one of our entertainers, you had to pass a very stringent test. Basically, you had to be awful at whatever you specialized in. Secondly, you had to have a regular attendance record.

Apparently to us kids, anyone that truly did well at his or her chosen form of ministry just didn't seem funny. For example, when Brother and Sister Harrell would stand on the platform to sing, we always cracked up. Regardless of the song they chose, they were never in the same key with one another. Neither did they manage to complete a whole verse without losing their places and having to start the entire verse over. No matter how hard I attempted to control my reaction to their scattered brain-clashing duets, Kenny's low rumbling laugh would always manage to get me going.

John Stevens was Dad's Sunday school superintendent and we loved for him to sing on Sunday mornings, because it always started the day off with a bang. John almost always sang solo and I can't remember him ever completing a single song. He would usually make it through about one half of the first verse before he would realize that the song was either to high or to low for him to sing it in the present key. This would usually result in his shaking his head back and forth from side to side while pursing his lips together and staring at his little black song book laid open on the pulpit. He would ultimately start laughing like a machine gun firing as he turned to the musicians to have them raise or lower the key and try again. He would often repeat this pattern as many as two to three times before finally giving up. He would then announce as a matter of fact, "Well, glory to God! The devil's gonna have to defeat me today. Everybody stand and go to your classes." By the time he finished trying nearly every musical key, he would dismiss the congregation to their respective places and Kenny and I would barely be able to walk as a result of our laughter.

We no doubt thought, "Where on earth could a good Christian get such incredible and improvisational comedy-- and for free?" It was never our intention to be sacrilegious or anything, we were just at the stage in life where everything gross is cool and everyone who messes up is funny.

Erica Blanch was one of my personal favorites. When she sang, she made Kenny feel uncomfortable and that was always good for a laugh. Now Blanch's mother considered herself a prophetess. Her name was Hilda. The Lord had shown Hilda that Erica and Kenny were destined to marry one another. Hilda made it perfectly clear to my mother that any attempt to divert from this providential course of action would result in God's anger and wrath. My mother never actually took this prophecy to be a reality I suppose, however, it made for some great ribbing on my part. Hilda liked to show off Erica's singing talents for Kenny's sake. When she would start singing, I would punch Kenny and remark, "There's the future Mrs. Kenny Hinson." Kenny didn't find my comments about Erica a bit funny and would usually jump up quickly and head straight to the rest room. "Hurry back," I would softly announce, as he departed for the men's room. "You don't want to miss this, she's singing just for you!" Kenny often stayed in the rest room until he figured that Erica was finished before returning to his seat.

Probably one of our all time favorite entertainers was Sister Ingram. Whenever Sister Ingram would sing a song like "Elijah Prayed," she strutted across the platform kicking her feet up towards the hem of her dress. At the same time, she bopped her head forwards and backwards like a chicken, while quickly jerking her neck and fluttering her fingers behind her back like ruffling feathers. This display of diverse motion was usually more than Kenny or I could handle, and we would burst out laughing with our heads lowered just below that back of the seat in front of us.

There were a number of times when our brother Ronny helped our cause by acting as a major contributor to the request list. Ronny had a very special way of lining up our roster of talent through the process of sending a note to the intended performer, asking them to come to the platform and sing. He would sign the note "Brother Hinson." Ronny figured that the recipient would naturally believe the request to have come from "The" Brother Hinson, our dad. It always seemed to work, so Kenny and I did everything in our power to encourage Ronny's involvement.

At this time Ronny became our father's youth pastor, so Ronny felt as though he had some level of authority to make requests anyhow. The really funny thing about the invitations to sing were that they would also notify the recipient that they should come to the platform immediately and start singing. As a result, the entertainer would come to the stage at once, regardless of what Dad or the superintendent had scheduled as the next event for the service. The singer would wind up preempting the agenda with a song. Ronny usually even told the singer which song he wanted them to present. This always helped ensure that the entertainment for the day was exceptionally good! Dad was usually looking down at his Bible, chewing on the inside of his lip and concentrating intensely on his sermon when one of the singers would mount the stage and start talking. Many times he looked up over his dark rimmed glasses in astonishment, surprised to discover who was preparing to deliver a song. His eyebrows would furl and his eyes would start scanning the congregation for Ronny's location in the sanctuary. Ronny had often endured the fire of Dad's gaze under similar circumstances, yet he relied heavily on his own humorous talents to free him from incurring dad's wrath. There were even a few occasions when Daddy covertly shook his fist at Ronny from behind the cover of his Bible as if to indicate that he would get him for this later. As the parishioners continued to ply their wares on the whole of the congregation, the shear awfulness of it all usually forced a small grin to Daddy's face. For Kenny and I to enjoy the pleasure of hearing such horrific singing was one thing, however, to watch our father reluctantly surrender to the urge to laugh was sheer delight! Once Daddy gave in to the overwhelming drive to smile, Ronny would immediately glance in our direction with a smirk of accomplishment pasted across his face.

Of course, the majority of the invitations went out to none other than Ramona Crown. Ramona Crown was a little petite woman from Louisiana that most likely stood no more than four feet two inches high. Like many of us, she didn't have very much money to speak of and so she bought most of her clothes at the local Goodwill Store. Ramona came to church from the discount store one time wearing a shimmering party dress from the nineteen fifties, featuring a plunging neck line and a low cut back with spaghetti straps. Being a holy and modest woman, she decided she would accessorize by adding a long sleeve loose knit sweater underneath the gown. Kenny and I laughed till tears ran down our cheeks as Ramona climbed to the platform wearing this get up, complete with clear plastic pumps that were to small for her feet and made her toes appear to be wrestling with one another. Ramona had very few teeth in the front of her mouth and for whatever reason always wore her hair pulled straight back in pony tail, which was held together by a single rubber band. Ramona loved to sing and had a tremendous passion for conversation. Kenny and I were always amazed at just how fast the woman could talk without ever stopping to catch her breath.

When it was her time to assume her surprising place behind the sacred desk you could barely see the top of her head from the congregation's vantagepoint. As she would begin her rendition, she would rear back her head and start pounding the palm of her right hand ever so softly against the podium. It was at this time that our entire group of believers truly experienced her full range of volume. She held nothing back as she belted out each word into the echoing auditorium. "One day religion just won't do, the Lord expects a week from you, if you wanna go up, ya godda go down brother and pray, ay, ay, ay. Be baptized in the wooter hole, that won't never, never save your soul, shake and shake the preacher's hand, that won't get ya to the promise land. Change your heart, change your mind, turn away and leave the world behind. If you wanna go up, ya godda go down, brother and pray, ay, ay, ay."

Sister Ramona's hillbilly tones certainly seemed funny enough on their own, but when she combined her talents with the interference from her kids, the entire escapade was completely hilarious. She always seemed to have her children Betty, Jennifer and Freddy present with her at church and many times she felt it necessary to stop singing right in the middle of a verse or chorus to correct one of her kids. It often sounded something like… "Be baptized in the wooter hole that won't never, never save your soul, Freddy, you better sit down and shut up or I'm coming back there, to whoop ya right now!" She would then proceed to look in the direction of the musicians, giggle and then continue from the very place she had left off as though there had been no interruption at all. "Shake and shake the preacher's hand, that won't get you to the promise land."

This kind of stuff was particularly enjoyable for Kenny and me. Once we asked her and her oldest daughter Jennifer to sing a song together, entitled "Blind Barnamas." While Sister Ramona was to sing the actual verses and choruses, Jennifer was supposed repeat her mother's words in a recital fashion, allowing each word to sort of lap over her mother' lines. If Kenny and I had been accumulating a top ten list of songs, this one would have no doubt been number one on the chart. Now you've got to keep in mind that Jennifer was a little on what one might call the rebellious side of religion in those days. As a matter of fact, from time to time Jennifer would slip out of service when no one was paying attention to join Carl Kelsey outside for a cigarette. Carl liked to sit out in front of the church in his 1949 Plymouth convertible listening to the local rock n' roll station, while his smoke loosely dangled from his lips and his right arm rested on the top of his gray cloth covered seat. Carl felt that because he was already eighteen years old that he should no longer be under the auspices of his mother. On the other hand, Jennifer was only sixteen and still considered a minor.

When Sister Ramona received a request to come to the platform and get ready to sing the favorite song on our private hit parade, she naturally started looking around for Jennifer. Jennifer was no place to be found in the sanctuary or bathroom. After a thorough search of the building failed to turn up any Jennifer, a look of both anger and frustration swept across Sister Ramona's face as she hastily made her way to the front door of the little storefront. Sure enough, when Sister Ramona opened the front door and stepped out onto the front steps, there stood Jennifer sharing a cigarette with Carl. As Jennifer stood puffing, giggling and leaning over the passenger's door in order to position her self almost directly in front of Carl's face, she never noticed as Ramona came up behind her. According to Betty, Jennifer's little sister who had followed hot on the heels of Sister Ramona as she hurried to find her daughter's whereabouts, Jennifer nearly swallowed her cigarette when her mom called her name from only one foot behind her.

Carl had the radio turned up nearly full blast in order to sing along with his favorite song, "Come On Baby Light My Fire." With his slicked back, pompadour hairstyle and the sleeves of his white v-necked T-shirt rolled up to expose his muscles, Carl sang loud as he took a drag off his Kool cigarette. With all the intentions of impressing his female audience, Carl had closed his eyes in order to appear extraordinarily passionate about the words for Jennifer's sake. He never noticed Ramona either, until it was too late.

The moment Sister Ramona shouted out Jennifer's name, Carl's cigarette fell out of his mouth and nearly caught his blue jeans on fire. Ramona kept striking Jennifer on the arm with a small switch the entire journey back into the auditorium, where she commenced to usher her up onto the platform for the duet. Jennifer was both angry and embarrassed. She was in no mood to be in front of the whole church, let alone sing for them. Those of us sitting near the open front door, accidentally left ajar by Betty in her attempt to accompany her mom to the crime scene, experienced the unique pleasure of hearing a great portion of the encounter.

To Kenny and I, this was more humorous and interesting than anything we could have watched on television. We clearly heard the unmistakable sounds of someone blurting out an occasional, "OOW!" directly following the smack of something abruptly contacting bare flesh. We were also certain that Jennifer was fully aware of the fact that many people had been privy to her personal discipline. Yet she knew she had to sing. Her mother read her the riot act and kept informing her on the way to the stage, "You'd better be repentin' girl, before you get up thare to sang! God don't want to hear someone sang who's just had a cigarette in their mouth without repentin' first."

For this reason, Jennifer had no intention of facing the congregation's direction while she sang. Instead, as Sister Ramona took her usual place behind the podium, Jennifer positioned herself to the right hand side of the desk, with her buttocks poked out and her knees locked in place. She rested her chin on the palm of her left hand as she placed her elbow firmly on top of the pulpit's wooden trim. Reluctantly and with a look of sheer boredom on her face, Jennifer began to accompany her mother's selection.

"This is gonna be even better than I thought!" Kenny softly announced in my right ear. Now I don't mean to leave the impression that Jennifer had been completely cooperative with her mother since being forced away from her perspective romance. She had already accomplished her fair share of griping and complaining, while being escorted up the aisle to the stage. As far as Kenny was concerned, that could only mean that this situation still had all the potential of becoming extremely explosive. Ramona turned in the direction of the musicians and spoke loudly, "I don't know what key this song's in, ya all will just have to try an folla." After a couple of attempts at locating a suitable key, Ramona let go at full volume. "Blind Barnamas." This was followed by a halfhearted, echoed recital from Jennifer, who was still in her bent over profile, tapping her fingers against her left cheek ever so dramatically. "Blind Barnamas said." Ramona continued, oblivious to the overtones of resentment exuding from Jennifer's words. "Cried out by the wayside." "Cried out by the wayside," came the repetitive lyrics, still carrying all the tell-tell signs of Jennifer's sarcastic intentions and no doubt a great desire for the song to end. No sooner had Ramona began singing the third line of the song than Kenny and I realized our fondest hopes. "And a voice spoke like thunder…" Ramona's words trailed off into oblivion as Jennifer decided it was time to get this over with quickly. Without warning, Jennifer had overlapped her mother's line before waiting on her mother to complete it. She then went on to finish the whole next line of the song, which culminated in an all out argument. "And a voice spoke like thunder, said this is my son."

"Hurry up, Mama, you're going to slow," Jennifer blurted.

Ramona fired back with anger in her tone. "I'm going just as fast as I can!"

"Well, that's not fast enough," Jennifer snarled. All at once an all out battle broke out between mother and daughter, complete with Ramona switching Jennifer off the platform and down to the altar to pray and ask God for forgiveness. Kenny and I cracked up laughing uncontrollably.

# CHAPTER FOUR

## GOODBYE WORLD, GOODBYE

It could easily be said that our dad was the source from which we drew our scriptural and spiritual hunger. On the other hand, it was mostly from Mom that we drew our vocal and musical talents. Dad was, in fact, quite the singer for his time. He often appeared on radio broadcasts with both my sister Barbara and sister Yvonne. However, Mom inspired us to learn how to play a musical instrument. Mom already played the piano, guitar and accordion and she possessed and incredible passion to teach her children those instruments as well. It was Mom who taught Kenny and me to play the guitar. She taught us where to place our fingers on the neck of the guitar to make a clear chord. My fingers were smaller than Kenny's were, and I had a difficult time standing them up to prevent the deadening of the strings. Kenny, however, was a natural. C, G, F, D and A were the very first chords that Mom taught us how to play.

Some of my other siblings, like Calvin, Barbara, Harold and Ronny, had already taken the "Stella Hinson" guitar course. Most of them had learned to play a good rhythm guitar, but Kenny alone seem to excel in this particular musical interest. He set his sights on playing lead guitar. By the time I was ten years old, Kenny was nearly thirteen and already starting to play lead guitar pretty well.

Kenny had fallen in love with the high twanging notes that exuded from the lead guitar talents of a young man visiting our church one night and was never again content to just play rhythm. Kenny became so determined to be as good a player as the young man he had witnessed at church that he found a couple of old records by Chet Atkins and Billy Grammer that he could listen to and attempt to duplicate. As if a light had gone off in his head, Kenny somehow knew that this musical talent he was in the process of acquiring would be directly connected to his destiny.

From that point on, all of Kenny's priorities seemed to change. Nothing seemed to be more important to Kenny than learning how to play professional lead guitar. Hour after hour he would sit in front of the old console stereo player, playing either his Billy Grammer record or the one by Chet Atkins. He would listen to a single musical run played by the artist, stop the record and place the needle and arm right back in the identical place and listen again. He would do this repeatedly, until everyone in the house was half crazy. He would then attempt time and time again to copy the musical maneuver until he finally got it down pat. I can't tell you how many times my mom would remind him to be careful with her turn table or needle. Almost everyday, directly after school Kenny would go into the closet and get out his old hand me down imitation Blue Swede box guitar and begin the process all over again. Even the time we were spending together at play had greatly diminished, since his newfound interest in playing the lead guitar. It seemed to make little difference to Kenny that his guitar lacked a good sound or appearance. Due to someone sanding down the finish until nothing showed but the blonde bare wood, most every tone that resounded from the almost miniature instrument seemed to lack the ability to sustain itself for more than a second or two. Kenny paid no attention, however, and just kept practicing to become the very best he could possibly be.

Kenny continued to fine tune his God given talents until one day he felt accomplished enough to join the other musicians on the platform at church. I really can't remember what Kenny's first electric guitar looked like or what the brand name was, but I am pretty certain that his first amplifier was a small Fender. Even after Kenny joined the little Brooklyn Street church house band, it still took him quite a long period of time before he was comfortable enough in his own talent, so that he could confidently increase the volume up beyond his own hearing range.

After several months of intense practice, Kenny began playing solos for the offering at the church. Two of his favorite songs were "The Lion of Judah" and "Goodbye World, Goodbye."

I began to see less and less of Kenny after school each day, while Steve Whurtley saw more and more. Steve was no doubt Kenny's best friend at the time and shared an interest in musical instruments as well. Steve played the bass guitar and often accompanied Kenny during one of his practice sessions at the church where Steve's dad was the pastor. It was only a couple of blocks away from our house, and Kenny loved the spaciousness and privacy that the Assembly of God church afforded. Together, the two of them had long afternoon jam sessions and eventually they entered a Christian talent contest together. When the two of them returned with first place trophy, Kenny seemed to be all aglow and filled with exuberance. Later that night, when everyone was in bed, Kenny and I quietly discussed the events of that day and he explained to me how good it felt to be on the stage before a large congregation performing.

"Man," I said, propping myself up on my left elbow, as I turned to face the direction from where I had last heard his voice through the darkness on the opposite side of the room. "That's so neat. I'll probably never know what that feels like."

"Larry, it was so cool, man!" Kenny spoke again while reaching over to click on the light. "I've never felt so happy as I did hearing that congregation clap their hands when me and Steve finished playing. I really feel like the guitar is part of what I'm supposed to do for God."

Little did either one of us realize that night just how much a part of his life and ministry that little wood stringed instrument would play. Nor did we foresee just how many lives that his passion for playing the guitar would ultimately effect. The truly strange thing about Kenny's playing was, the more confident he became in his guitar talent, the more comfortable he became with his vocal abilities. Mom soon suggested the two of us put together some duets while Kenny played the guitar simultaneously. The members of the little church really seemed to enjoy our special numbers. We eventually wound up becoming regulars on the roster of entertainers each week.

During this same period of time, Ronny discovered and became a fan of southern gospel music. Ronny traveled all over California to hear different groups perform. Groups like the Stamps Quartet, Blackwood Brothers and The Happy Goodman Family drew him from city to city in effort to hear them perform. It is at this point in time that Ronny was working some with Brother Frank Polumbo. Brother Polumbo was the pastor of a little Church of God church located in the town of Freedom.

One night during December, Ronny invited the family to come over to the revival services conducted by John Rhodes and Harold Flannery. These two Pentecostal evangelists were working together as a team and alternating back and forth as the evening speaker. Ronny insisted that we attend the meeting, telling us about the great signs and wonders that had transpired during the services. We were extremely excited about the different miracles we witnessed and the powerful singing and preaching the team demonstrated each night.

Kenny and I were incredibly impressed by the way this duo made their entrance onto the stage. When they arrived in the auditorium each evening, they brandished briefcases and sported full-length trench coats, complete with towels about their necks. No doubt the towels were present in the great anticipation of the hot time in the Holy Ghost we would be having as the evening progressed. It was our first occasion to see anything so flamboyant. Coming from a background where men and women often made it a point to warn the audience not to look at them while they ministered but rather to see the Jesus in them.

"How cool!" Kenny whispered, as John Rhodes passed only inches from where we were setting. In those days, revival meetings didn't last the typical four days they do today. Many of them went a minimum of two weeks. We had chosen to attend an old fashioned, Spirit filled, Holy Roller meeting during that winter of 1967. Even though there were certainly a good number of healings and miracles, the emphasis seemed primarily focused on salvation and the baptism into the Holy Spirit. I had been filled with the Spirit since I was five years old and readily evidenced it by speaking in an unknown tongue as the Spirit gave the utterance. Kenny had yet to experience the infilling and was growing more and more anxious as the revival drew closer to the day of its conclusion.

Night after night, people were shouting, speaking in tongues and dancing in the Holy Ghost, some even falling out under the influence of God's Spirit. Kenny witnessed this with tears of envy running down his flushed cheeks. Often he would longingly look around the little humid auditorium at others experiencing the wonderful benefits of such a powerful atmosphere. He wept and cried out with desire for his own experience in the Spirit.

I'll never forget his words to me one night as one of the services was winding down during the revival. Kenny looked at me with such a sad expression on his face. Tears welled up in his eyes and his voice cracked as he spoke. "I want the Holy Ghost so bad Larry, but I don't know what to do to get it. I don't want it to be me," he explained, while placing the palms of his hands over his closed eyes. "I truly want it to be God that I feel and not me. Man, Larry," Kenny went on, "I envy you so much." He hung his head down, slowly shaking it from side to side, as if to ask God the question, "Why not me?" He started to say more but his words seemed to trail off into a kind of sobbing sound, as he now cupped his hands over both his mouth and eyes.

"Kenny," I said in a voice intended to sound reassuring. "You're gonna get it man, just hang in there." He lifted his eyes slowly from their buried position and looked directly at me as if he needed to plead his case before God.

"Larry," his voice broke again as he pressed the tissue against his nostrils. "I know I'm called to preach and if I could just get the Holy Ghost, man, I know I could preach the way God wants me to." All at once he started sobbing again, his eyes spurting water like a fountain. "I'm so scared, man." He said, his voice now lowering to a whisper.

"What are you scared about?" I questioned with a genuine tone of concern as I placed a hand on his shoulder to comfort.

"I'm scared that God won't give it to me."

"God's no respecter of persons!" I said as a matter of fact, while waving my hand in the air.

"Yeah," Kenny interjected. "Easy for you to say, you've always been so bold. Why, even the very first time you got up to preach, you were completely confident in yourself."

"No Kenny!" I interrupted, now placing my hand on his knee for emphasis. "I'm just confident in God." It was true that I had preached my first sermon at my daddy's church earlier that summer and that just a few weeks later I preached my first camp meeting at Beulah Park in Santa Cruz. It was a wonderful meeting with over thirty kids, my age and younger, saved and filled with the Holy Ghost. I knew I was self-assured, but only because I genuinely believed that if God called you, He equipped you for the job. I could tell that Kenny felt as if he was being left out while his little brother was being greatly used of God.

It would actually be some eleven years later that Kenny would finally come to experience his personal infilling of the Holy Spirit. That precious event would ultimately transpire behind my chocolate brown velvet sofa in Hendersonville, Tennessee. It was there, lying on the floor during one of our many prayer meetings together in the 1970s, that Kenny came to realize God had not excluded him after all!

Kenny was elated during the course of the revival however, when he discovered that the evangelists wanted him to play his guitar for the congregation. Excited and yet somewhat frightened by the concept of performing before such anointed and talented musicians, Kenny brought his guitar to church and offered the crowd a sample of his playing. Once again, Kenny fell back on what he came to relate to as "Old Faithful," "Goodbye World, Goodbye." The song inevitably raised a shout of hallelujahs from the exuberant band of believers. When Kenny stepped from the platform, the applause seemed to carry him back to his seat like he was floating on a cloud. I was never so proud of my big brother, and something inside me longed to be a part of his great talent. I comforted myself in the thought of singing duets with him, like Mama had initiated.

It was during this same revival that the Hinsons were asked to come to the platform and sing. First we sang as individuals and duets and then ultimately all together as a family. It was there on December 12, 1967, that we officially sang our first song as a group. Out of all the gospel groups that Ronny had managed to expose us to over the many months, The Happy Goodman Family seemed to impress us most of all. To us, they seemed like a family unit similar to ours and basically from the same Pentecostal background. Needless to say, theirs was the kind of music we listened to most on records and their songs were the ones we most easily remembered. So whenever we were asked to sing a song collectively, we chose a Goodman number. "The Eyes of Jesus" was our favorite song and so it was only fitting that we performed the song that made us feel the most blessed when we sang it.

Kenny had long been a fan of country music entertainers like Merle Haggard. Yet when he stepped to the microphone and opened his mouth to sing, more of a conventional country sound flowed from his lips. The audience immediately burst into shouts of praise and worship unto the Lord! We became such a favorite in the little country church that we were invited back the remaining nights to sing again.

This, Ronny decided, required some rehearsal. After all, we pretty much only knew the one song, and we would naturally have to learn more. We needed to get organized with some kind of a repertoire. We also needed an official name for our group. Initially, we called ourselves The Galileans, until we discovered the name was already the property of a professional group from Dallas, Texas. We finally came to call ourselves The Singing Hinson Family, an admittedly similar sounding name to our gospel music idols. Kenny, who was normally shy and unimposing, seemed to find strength and boldness as he stood behind the body of his six-string companion. He was already realizing that the next phase of this ministry would require much more than simply an ability to play "Goodbye World, Goodbye."

After the revival and our newly discovered talents, Ronny began to suggest that we enter some talent contests and get his long time friend Carl Harvell to play the bass guitar for us. Although we lacked any adequate instruments or sound equipment, Ronny and Carl soon persuaded a local music store to sponsor us with the necessary items. For most of us, the concept of singing as a gospel group and entering gospel talent contests seemed exciting. For Kenny, however, it only meant more practice and not just on his guitar, but his vocal performance as well. If he was going to get up in front of people judging his talents, he was determined to be good!

# CHAPTER FIVE

## A PROMISE TO BE NUMBER ONE

After the initial realization that we might just have something special to offer as a singing group, Ronny saw fit to drag us up and down the west coast in pursuit of winning a gospel music talent contest. Perhaps he felt that winning was a necessary symbol of excellence and acceptance in order to officially become a full-fledged southern gospel group. The only problem was, we never won anything we entered. We didn't even qualify.

In one particular location, one of the talent contest judges basically advised us that we should throw in the towel and go home. Eventually, however, doors began to open on a completely different and unexpected level. Pastors from different churches in our area starting showing an interest in us and asked us if we would minister at their churches. Word got around I guess, and over the next couple of years, more and more pastors booked engagements with us.

Although we may not have been good enough to win any talent contests at the time, we eventually found ourselves smack dab in the middle of a recording contract with Calvary Records based out of Fresno. The producer heard us sing at a concert in Salinas and asked us to sign with him. Our first two projects on the Calvary label were called "Here Come The Hinsons" and "Gospel Sound Spectacular." Neither one of our first two albums seemed to raise even the slightest bit of envy from the local southern gospel groups, let alone any recognition from the professional sector. In reality, we had not yet found our notch in gospel music.

It was extremely advantages for The Singing Hinson Family that the individual promoting most of the west coast southern gospel concerts just so happened to be our record producer as well. We naturally found ourselves opening for many of the more popular performers, which gave us the prestige of singing in many of the large concert halls and auditoriums in central and northern California.

We soon began to dream about becoming one of the hottest groups that ever hit the big time! And of course, if you're going to play with the big boys, then you've got to have a bus to travel in. What big time group traveled in a van? One of the tell-tell signs of a local group was the vehicle they drove to the concert in. If they pulled into the parking lot driving a motor home or pulling a trailer behind a car, you knew immediately that they were a "local yokel" group. On the other hand, if they drove in sporting a nicely painted bus, then a major group had just arrived on the scene!

You cannot imagine the elation that Kenny and I experienced the day we first stepped foot on our own bus. In those days, you didn't dare insult the integrity of owning your own personal symbol of success by calling it simply a bus. No, quite the contrary. To properly identify your status of religious nobility with regard to your vehicle of transport, you would always refer to it as a "Private Coach."

Kenny and I immediately started using the terminology, shortly after boarding the first time. It made no difference to us that the 1948 Greyhound Silverside bore evidence of many years of wear and tear. To us, it was the necessary ingredient for being successful in gospel music.

When we first picked the coach up, it had been used as a school bus and was still painted school bus yellow. Although we realized we would have to wait a little while before raising enough money to paint it another color, this did nothing to dampen our spirits. By the time we finally drove the bus home, it was already dark outside. While our brother Harold took hold of the helm, steering us safely in the direction of Salinas, Kenny and I headed down the aisle towards the rear of the bus. The two us decided to try out our bus legs and quickly discovered how hard it was to stay standing while the coach was moving. We took turns falling down and then laughing at each other. We finally decided to take a couple of seats in the very back, far enough away from the rest of the crowd now sitting in the front rows and begin our daydreams about where our rooms might be located. We even discussed what they would eventually look like.

"I want my bunk to be right over the engine," Kenny said with an air of excitement in his voice. "That way, the engine noise will just hum me to sleep."

"Me too!" I said, thinking to myself, wherever Kenny goes that's where I want to be.

"I've got dibs on the bottom bunk," Kenny announced abruptly, as if the beds were already built and the covers were already pulled back.

"That's okay," I replied shrugging my shoulders in a display of unconcern. "I like the top bunk better anyway."

"Can you believe it, Larry?" Kenny asked with a goggle-eyed expression. "We've got a bus!"

"Wow!" I responded, feeling as if I had just received the news that I had become a millionaire.

Kenny just kept on ranting over the concept of finally looking professional. "It's hard to believe, isn't Larry? It's really ours!"

"Yeah!" I exclaimed in a tenor of pure delight.

"No more sitting in the stupid utility van on metal folding chairs that fall over every time we turn a corner, or when we're taking off or stopping," Kenny went on to explain. "Just think about it, Larry. No more hairspray in the face." I knew exactly what Kenny was talking about. When we traveled in the old van and were just about ready to arrive at our date, the girls would start pulling out their hairbrushes and hairspray. The inside of the already cramped quarters would become even more cramped, as the atmosphere began to get thick and sticky from the fog of aerosol Final Net permeating everything insight. By the time they finished heavily shellacking their beehive hair dos, we could hardly breathe. Kenny and I would look over at each other shaking our heads in disbelief, as we covered our noses with the curved front neckline of our t-shirts. "Just imagine, Larry," Kenny declared, "after a concert we can come back here to our room, shut the door and talk, listen to the radio or whatever."

"Kenny?" I spoke now in an almost timid tone.

"Yeah?" Kenny replied as if to permit a question he knew I was destined to ask.

"Do you remember the prophecy we received about becoming the number one group in the nation?"

"Yeah," Kenny's reply was almost a whisper now.

"Do you think that is ever really going to happen?"

"I don't know," Kenny shrugged his shoulders and raised his eyebrows slightly. His tone seemed to be laced with a touch of frustration as well. "I hope so, but who can be sure?"

"Maybe it will happen," I suggested cautiously.

"Well!" Kenny suddenly remarked as if having just received insight into the future. "It probably will. After all, God keeps his promises. Besides, if God did it for other groups, then he can do it for us!" And with that, I determined in my heart that Kenny was probably right about the prophecy coming true, and that we would no doubt become the number one gospel group someday.

Little did I know that the someday was just a little over a decade away. I never realized then that Kenny would play one of the major roles in bringing about that promise either. Yet, just two years later, life for the Hinsons would dramatically change.

By the summer of 1970, Ronny, Harold and Carl made the decision to leave their secular jobs and hit the road full time. Kenny and I were out of school for the summer and Yvonne was eager to put a bad relationship behind her quickly. The Hinson Family found themselves making their very first eastern tour across the United States that summer.

We only had fifty dollars, an ice chest full of lunchmeat items and a whole lot of either faith or pure ignorance to last us the entire journey. The way we saw it, because we would be singing at different locations along the way there would be plenty of offerings taken to sustain us throughout the trip.

The only problem was, when we were barely into the tour Donna, Carl's little two-year old daughter, inadvertently made a toilet out of the ice chest. The food was completely ruined and what little money we had started out with was quickly depleted by the necessity of frequent fuel stops and some mechanical difficulties with the old Silverside. At one point, each of us guys took turns running behind the old coach spraying ether into its intake vents. We were right out in the middle of the dessert where there was nothing and no one to assist us. We had to keep forcing the ether into clogged fuel lines in order to keep the engine going a little further. At least until we came to a service station or something.

We would run along behind the bus, spray the ether and then sprint to catch up and jump aboard. It was imperative that we did nothing to prevent the engine from reaching our desired goal, so we kept alternating runners until we finally spotted a truck stop nestled in between some mountain ranges. We had prayed and prayed for somewhere to stop and fix the fuel lines, and when we finally spotted the truck stop, it was like a thirsty caravan discovering an oasis.

We attempted to locate that same truck stop several times after our initial crossing. Whenever we passed through that area we inquired about its location, but we never found it again. We even mentioned to some truckers about having some engine work done at the truck stop only hours after our repairs. We were promptly informed that there was nothing even remotely resembling a truck stop in that part of the dessert. Perhaps, God does place an oasis in dry places after all!

It was nearly one hundred and seventeen degrees in the shade when we finally arrived in Prescott, Arizona that summer. It was so hot that the tops of my feet were burning right through my tennis shoes. As usual, our bus broke down and so did the air conditioner. Everyone was miserable because of the extreme heat and heavy humidity that hung in the air like a shroud. We were completely out of money and our only option was to pray for relief from both the heat and the hunger.

I can still remember hearing Kenny talking to the Lord during one of our many group prayer meetings that grueling summer. "Lord," Kenny whispered, "we're hungry, Lord, and it's hot here. We need your help, God," he stated with a wisp of desperation to his tone. "Please do something to help us. We're just trying to do your work, Lord." For a moment, I felt a little guilty for listening in on his private conversation with God. I knew I should have been praying, too instead of eavesdropping, however, Kenny was always so sincere in everything he did. No doubt, because he never wanted anything to be a result of his own fleshly desires and therefore always went to great lengths to search his soul for the right attitude when doing something for the Lord. If anyone was going to touch God's heart, I decided in my mind, it would be Kenny. I finally came to the conclusion that God was listening to Kenny's prayer as well and that all I had to say was "Amen!"

Here we were waiting on an opportunity to get on to the program at the Youth Conference International, a newly developed annual fellowship that was making its debut in Prescott. We had been promised the chance to sing at the Pentecostal Church of God Conference, but mostly we were being ignored. We had been waiting for some news from our record producer, a well-known leader in the organization, as to whether we would sing or not. At the time, we needed a comfortable place to stay and just the thought of a cool shower sounded heavenly.

Finally, my brother Harold who was driving for us that summer, told us he had hidden a little extra cash away for his own personal rainy day, so to speak. I suppose that his conscience had gotten the best of him as he continued to witness the increasing desperation within the group. "So," Kenny muttered sarcastically, "been holding out on us, have you?" Kenny now used a humorous tone, complete with an intentional slur to his words. Everyone knew however that Kenny was only halfway kidding. Harold went on to explain his reasons for not sharing what little money he had remaining and how he could not possibly maintain such expenditures for any length of time. It was enough to buy some more lunchmeat and condiments and even a few bottles of some Royal Crown Cola.

The next day a man from the conference came along and offered to fix our bus for just the cost of the parts. When he stated that he would start by pulling out the carburetor from the diesel engine, Harold realized that this gentleman knew absolutely nothing about working on a bus engine.

Finally a fellow Californian, a pastor from Visalia, came by under what he called "instructions from the Lord." He placed some money in Harold's hand and told him to get the bus fixed. It was just enough Kenny told me later, as he informed me of the good news. "We're gonna be able to get out of here after all!" he exclaimed with delight.

In the meantime, our record producer had managed to make arrangements for us to be on the Y.C. I. program that night. The Happy Goodman Family was rumored to be there as well.

"Larry," Kenny blurted out as he wiped the sweat from his dripping forehead with the back of his right hand, "we're going to get to sing on the same program with the Goodmans!"

"I'm nervous!" I confided.

"Don't be nervous. This could be the break we've been waiting for!" Kenny announced his perspective with prophetic insight as we stepped from beneath the heat-conducting exterior of the bus into the cool interior of a side hallway leading to the auditorium's showers. The minute we became guests of the Y.C.I. leadership, our status jumped up a notch or two. Not only were we permitted to shower in the building, we were suddenly allowed to place our instruments on the stage and set our one and only record rack up in the lobby of the auditorium.

Finally when the evening service started, we hurried to put our stage clothes on and rushed to the wings of the platform. We were in great anticipation of our time in the limelight that night. Kenny and I didn't seem to notice that our royal blue cuff-linked dress shirts and white ties (complete with matching swank tie tacks) were nearly soaked from perspiration. We were just plain ecstatic over the thought of being on the same program with our idols of gospel music! Still not really sure how this sort of thing really worked, we just stood around fully dressed, waiting to go on at a moment's notice, while Carl and Kenny kept their instruments strapped about their necks everywhere that went back stage.

"Come 'ere, Come 'ere, Come 'ere!" Kenny said in rapid succession, while motioning me over to him. He was standing at the entrance to one of the three wings of curtains holding the suspended material tightly between his left thumb and index finger. Kenny peeked around the edge of the material, as if he were attempting to keep his current activities completely covert. "It's them!" Kenny spoke in such a loud whisper that it was barely a whisper at all. He was so excited that he was having a difficult time containing his exuberance. He must have realized just how loud his momentary announcement had seemed and jerked his head back behind the curtain almost simultaneously with his statement.

"It's who?" I asked with confusion.

"It's them, the Happy Goodmans!" Kenny declared in a hushed tone, as he once again peered from behind the curtain in the direction of the superstars. When I managed to get Kenny to let go of his vantage point long enough for me to catch a glimpse, I immediately recognized Howard and Vestal Goodman sitting in the two folding chairs facing the stage. I couldn't believe we were really that close to them. "Larry," Kenny proclaimed softly, as he once again took possession of the outer edge of curtain I had just been peeping from. "What if they think we stink?" He turned away with an expression of genuine worry encompassing his face.

"I hope not!" I replied with a feeling of concern beginning to weight my thoughts. "Surely not?" I finally managed to exclaim. Kenny started strumming the strings on his guitar ever so lightly as he turned away and began to pace up and down behind the large curtain that served as the backdrop to the stage. He never spoke of it again that night but I could tell that he was plenty worried about their distain for our singing and was struggling with his own down cast feelings.

When it finally came our time to go on, we joined hands and reminded God of his promise to make us number one. We did our very best that night to act and sound professional.

When they eventually announced our name to the jam-packed crowd of Pentecostals, the applause was moderate at best. Kenny had always taken the attitude, "You may not like us when we first come out, but you're gonna want us to stay when it comes time for us to leave the stage."

By the time we got to a song made popular by the gospel music icons we had previously been spying on, the unexpected happened. All at once in the middle of our rendition to "I Found A Better Way," Vestal cried out in a loud voice for all to hear back stage. "That's Goodman singing!" With that, she and Howard joined us on the microphones for the remainder of the song. It just so happened that I brandished the lead vocal on that particular number, so Vestal stood with me while Howard took a position with Kenny at his stand. Ronny was unfortunately stuck with the General Superintendent of the organization, who was administering a rather awful sounding bass line into Ronny's ear. After that little endorsement by what we considered to be the royalty of gospel music, the Hinsons were simply the hit of the ball, if you know what I mean. Even the girls suddenly started noticing Kenny and I that evening. We both had good-looking girl friends for the rest of the conference. We had never signed so many autographs in our short career!

"Well!" Kenny announced to me privately in a affirming tone, as we drove away from the conference for the last time that week. "I think we're gonna see that promise come true, Larry."

I nodded my head in a sign of total agreement. "Yeah, we'll be number one before you know it."

# CHAPTER SIX

## NIGHTMARE ON ZOE STREET

We continued our tour across the eastern part of America, and we eventually found ourselves ministering in the large city of Houston, Texas. It was during one of our little church house meetings there that we ran into a nephew of one of Mama's old friends. The nephew's last name was Baker and he was the pastor of a fairly large church in the area. Realizing that our air conditioner was on the blink, he offered to let us stay at his church in an upstairs area where several classrooms were situated. He allowed us to park our bus in the parking lot and bring our mattresses into the facility.

Pastor Baker informed us that there was one double hide a bed in his office, but the rest of us would have to make do with a little less convenience. In the short ride from the church where we had been ministering to the church where we would be staying made us feel as if we were melting. The irony of it all was that we had managed to finally get the bus painted blue and white. Above the lone passenger door entering into the coach's interior were the words "Air Conditioned." Not only was it a really stupid idea and usually only posted on commercial buses, it simply wasn't true most of the time.

"It will feel so good to get out of this heat," Kenny said with a sigh of relief.

"No joke," I responded, rapidly fluttering the collar on the blue dress shirt that I was still wearing from the singing. We were all tired and hot. The long service and the sticky atmosphere left us feeling tremendously drained.

I followed closely behind Kenny through the single glass door, which led directly into the bottom level of the church's annex. The lower level also appeared to have several Sunday school classes on both sides of the long corridor, near the pastor's personal study.

Several times over the years, I have watched various documentaries of ragged looking refugees carrying what little belongings or bedding that they might still possess, in a desperate attempt to flee from the clutches of some dictator's political tyrannies. Looking back on that night, I realize that we must have made a similar impression on the pastor of that Pentecostal church as we stood single file, waiting to walk through the door carrying our bedding over our shoulders and our clothing flung over our arms. Everyone was looking pretty worn and haggard, as we eventually made the final trip back to the bus for the remaining luggage.

Carl, Mary and little Donna claimed the pastor's study as their own personal room. No one really felt cheated about the decision, since Donna was still so young and Mary was sick. As for the rest of us, it was upstairs to the classrooms. At first the steps went straight upward and then made an abrupt right turn. At the top of the staircase, a door with a little square window, much like one that could be found in a secular classroom, caught our attention. Kenny was in the lead and paused for moment before opening the door to peer through the crisscrossing wire that reinforced the pane. When we entered the upstairs annex, we were greeted by several rows of church pews, each one about twelve to fifteen feet in length and covering almost the entire area. It was sort of like a mini auditorium.

"Must be a children's church," Kenny said with a curious expression.

"Looks like it," I slowly replied, still feeling the effects of the sultry summer evening. Yvonne had already selected a room on the far right end of the long big room. Ronny and his family were in the room at the far right side, next to Yvonne's. Harold had picked a room about three doors up from the far end of the large space, on the left side. Kenny and I had decided to choose the room at the far-left end, directly opposite Yvonne's room.

The only thing that separated our two doors was a large black upright piano, openly displaying its yellowed ivory keys that were badly out of tune. At the far end of the room we had entered and directly to the right was a large bay window over looking the parking lot where our bus was parked.

Since being in the Houston area, we had acquired a brand new musician to the group. Carl had made it clear that the road life was far too difficult for him and his family and that he simply was not willing to make all the necessary sacrifices it required. So we brought in Jerry Seelea to take Carl's place. Jerry was both an accomplished rhythm guitarist and a bass guitarist as well. He was young enough and unmarried, which afforded him the opportunity to take a big risk economically.

When the three of us initially entered the upstairs area, we had felt extremely spent. But the cool, dry atmosphere provided us some newfound energy. Soon we rediscovered our sense of humor and ultimately lapsed into a giggling session that would last for several hours.

We had spent very little time at the place before we realized how hungry we were. Even so, we would eventually go to bed hungry that night. Yet the turn of events that transpired next literally made us forget about our gnawing bellies. We had been down in the sanctuary of the building for a couple hours, playing on instruments and just having a good time jamming. Finally we grew more sleepy than hungry and decided it was time to make our way back upstairs to our selected quarters. Even though we were tired enough to call it a night, more giggling soon erupted and we had to attempt to keep it down so that we wouldn't wake everyone.

The more we tried to control our laughter, the more we lost the ability to remain quiet. Jerry led the pack heading up the first flight of steps to our room giggling like a little girl. Kenny was directly behind him chuckling as well and I was bringing up the rear.

All at once, Jerry lost his balance and stumbled backwards, plowing in to Kenny and slamming him hard against the stairwell's wall. It felt as if the whole building shook from the impact and yet no one seemed to stir, not even Carl and his family who were only a few feet below us. "We'd better be quiet!" Kenny cautioned, placing his right index finger over his puckered lips. Once we tiptoed into our room, we still found it hard to stop clowning around and telling jokes. After about twenty minutes or so, we finally started settling down and giving over to some much-needed rest.

All at once we heard a loud, but somewhat distant crash. It didn't sound at all like a car crash or an airplane crash, but it had the unique sound of a cymbal crashing. More like a cymbal falling over to be exact. "Aah!" Kenny's voice blurted out, temporarily forcing our attention away from the noise. "Larry, you were the one playing the drums, did you move them somehow?"

"No!" I said in protest while rising up off my pillow simultaneously and turning to face his silhouetted face. "I promise, I didn't do anything that would cause them to fall over." I lifted my right hand, with my palm out to emphasize my honesty.

"Well, you had to do something!" Now his voice sounded rather accusatory from where I was lying. "They don't just fall over by themselves. You're the one who played them last and you're gonna have to be the one who goes down and straightens them up."

"Okay," I reluctantly replied, while producing a heavy sigh. I had just thrown back the covers in order to stand up and get my pants on, when all at once an equally disturbing noise pierced the moment of silence. Someone was now banging on the keys of the piano in the sanctuary.

Kenny sat up quickly, propped himself up on his right elbow and asked us in an obviously frightened tone, "Did you hear that?" We immediately realized that the piano wasn't the upright one sitting just outside our door. No, this was definitely coming from down stairs. Kenny turned his head in the direction where Jerry was lying and in that instant the light that had been behind him and obscuring his facial features shown directly on the side of his face just bright enough to reveal his wide eyes and gapping mouth. Kenny was visibly shaken by what we had heard and so were Jerry and I.

"Oh, my God!" Kenny said abruptly, while snapping his head in my direction. "Some kids or bums must have broken into the church and are tearing up the instruments in the sanctuary." What Kenny had suggested seemed relatively feasible.

We knew the neighborhood was a fairly rough one and for all we knew, that sort of thing might happen all the time around there. In our minds, it stood to reason that if we ran down stairs making enough of a racket, we might just be able to frighten the intruders away. "Okay," Kenny stated while jumping out of bed and flicking on the light. "Let's get dressed and then on the count of three, run down the stairs, flip on the lights in the downstairs corridor, then shout and clap as loud as we can, as we run towards the sanctuary." Jerry and I nodded quickly in a gesture of agreement.

We decided to be as quiet as possible as we went past the other rooms where the rest of the group was still asleep. "All right," Kenny mumbled as he opened our bedroom door and we stepped out into the larger room where the massive benches sat. He lowered his voice to a whisper. "No noise until we shut the stairwell door behind us." Again, Jerry and I nodded our compliance and then fell in behind him single file.

Slowly we traipsed past the room where Harold was sleeping directly on our right. The loud sound of snoring echoed from behind the wall, as we carefully trudged on. Kenny cautiously opened the heavy door with the little square window that led to the stairwell we had traversed in laughter only moments before. He carefully placed one foot in front of the other as he slowly made his way down the flight of stairs. Jerry followed next and once again I brought up the rear. I had no sooner closed the door behind me when, as if on cue, we heard the most clamorous crashing sound.

"We've gotta go in there," Kenny said with an air of dread in his voice, followed by a deep sigh.

"Let's go!" Jerry and I insisted. When our feet finally landed at the bottom of the stairs, we forgot all about Carl and his family right next to us in the pastor's office. We each let out with a loud yelp and starting clapping our hands together. It reminded me of some wild Indians on the warpath in some old time western movie. We ran down the corridor banging on the walls and even beating on the side of the metal drinking fountain, next to the glass door we had entered the building through earlier. When we rounded the corner leading down the final hallway towards the dark wood paneled doors that opened into the sanctuary, a strange feeling swept over us. The small, globed light hanging overhead cast an eerie shadow on the walls.

"All right!" Kenny suddenly announced sternly, as he took hold of the brass handle and pulled the right door open. "Larry, you go in first and find the light switch."

Suddenly, I wasn't sure if I wanted Kenny to be my military commander any longer. "Why me?" I asked with an air of protest.

"Because you can find the switch and we'll protect you," Kenny spoke with a tone of confidence in his voice, but I wasn't buying.

"How are you going to protect me, if you're still out here, while I'm in there?" My voice was obviously shaking from fear.

"Just go now!" Kenny blurted out, like a sergeant ordering his troops into battle. I knew that I was the only one who vaguely remembered where the light switch for the platform was located, but I didn't relish the idea of rushing head long into the pitch black room. Nonetheless, I did not want to appear frightened in front of either Kenny or Jerry. So I darted through the door and to the left as fast as possible.

Although my eyes had not had time to adjust to the darkened auditorium, I purposely started veering left until I smacked into the wall with my left shoulder. Next, I placed my left palm flat against the spackled wall and attempted to feel along its rough texture until my fingers made contact with the light switch. Something snapped behind me and quickly spun my head to the right in a blind attempt to see where the noise had come from.

All at once, for just a moment, my fingers felt the cold smooth surface of the plastic faceplate on the light switch. Then something struck me straight across my shins and I stumbled forward and fell on my face. For a second or two, I thought someone had tripped me on purpose in order to get the best of me. Just as quickly, I remembered there were stairs leading up to the switch and I had simply ran into the lowest one and caused my own fall.

I quickly picked myself up off the carpeted step and flicked the light switch on. As soon as I turned around in expectation of seeing instruments sprawled out across the stage, my peripheral vision caught the movement of Kenny and Jerry entering the room. By the look on their faces, I could tell that they were just as astonished at what they were seeing as I was. Absolutely, positively nothing had been moved. Kenny turned his head slowly in my direction. Both his eyebrows were bristled, directly above his two fear ridden eyes.

Kenny swallowed hard and looked at Jerry next. "What's going on here?" he asked in a tone of disbelief. Jerry shrugged his shoulders, as he lifted both palms of his hands upward to signify his confusion.

"They may have had time to stand the cymbals back up," I suggested, as I quickened my pace in the direction of the drums. "Let's see if they are in their original spots." I took hold of each one of the cymbals and every single drum and lifted them up. I wanted to see if they were resting in their original carpet indentations.

"Well?" Kenny impatiently questioned.

"They're good," I shouted. "If someone knocked them over, he was able to put them right back in their exact spot again."

Kenny rubbed his chin with his left thumb and forefinger, then slowly raised his head and spoke to Jerry. "You don't think we heard something happening outside our bedroom window do you?" His question seemed like a plausible explanation and yet certain elements didn't fit into the hypothesis.

Before Jerry could answer, I quickly interjected my opinion. "Okay, maybe you can explain away what sounded like a cymbal falling over, but a piano?"

Kenny suddenly blinked his eyes, like someone who just caught a speck of dirt in them. To me, it was an apparent indication that he agreed with my reasoning. "All right!" Kenny barked. "Let's check for unlocked doors leading from the sanctuary to the outside. I'll take this door here, Jerry take the far back right door and Larry check the foyer."

"Great!" I immediately thought. "Once again, Larry gets to check out the dark room." Kenny was still checking the integrity of the thumb press door handle on the exit door when I approached the blackened lobby. First it would be necessary for me to pass through the two swinging doors, each with a glass porthole that reminded me of two dark eyes. And speaking of eyes, I wasn't so sure if there weren't a couple of eyes watching me right at that moment from the other side of the doors. Cautiously, I pushed open the right-hinged door with my right hand. Carefully I peered into the shadow filled foyer half looking for a light switch and half looking for a person. Looking to my left was easy enough. I could clearly see that there was nothing on that side of the little lobby except a bare wall and a little entrance table. Looking to my right, however, presented a bit of a problem. I would have to step into the darkness and peek around the corner. That meant that whoever or whatever might be lurking in the blackened recesses of the room, could very easily get the jump on me.

I finally managed to raise enough courage to push myself forward and around the corner. As I stood still for a moment allowing my eyes to adjust to the darkness, I could immediately make out the figure of someone or something long and extremely dark standing directly in front of me. My heart leaped into my throat and I almost let out with a scream. Just then I recognized the object as nothing more than a forgotten trench coat, left over from some bygone winter. "All clear!" I shouted, as I once again walked through the port-holed doors and back into the sanctuary.

"Oh, well," Kenny announced, while slapping his hands against either thigh. "I guess it was just our imaginations or something." We headed back upstairs. We still felt strange about the whole ordeal, and when we reached the foot of the steps leading back up to our room, Carl cracked open the door to the pastor's study and peeked out, barely exposing a thin line of his face.

"You guys are gonna have keep it down out there. Mary's real sick," Carl whispered.

"We're sorry," Kenny said sincerely. "But didn't you hear all those cymbals crashing and the piano playing?" Kenny's question forced Carl to open the door and step out of his room. He closed the door quietly behind him. Carl was still squinting from the bright lights of the corridor.

"Yes," Carl said in a confused manner. "I did hear something like that, but I just thought it was you guys messing around."

"No!" Kenny blurted. " We could have sworn that somebody was down here tearing the instruments up, so we came down making all kinds of noise to scare them off."

"How strange," Carl replied while running his fingers through his mussed hair. "Well," Carl finally stated, "you boys had better go back up stairs and try and get some sleep."

"Okay," Kenny nodded, turning to face the staircase again. So once again we went back up stairs and attempted to go sleep.

The next morning was sunny and extremely humid. Once again, our thoughts turned to hunger as we got up, showered and prepared for the day. If memory serves me correctly, we were planning on consuming the traditional bologna and bread for our breakfast. Jerry was up long before Kenny and I and was currently no place to be found. Deciding that we would eat first, we checked out the new ice chest and discovered there was nothing in it.

"Maybe someone has gone to get some food and bring it back for the ice chest," I suggested.

"Maybe," Kenny replied in an almost depressed sounding tone. "But I know what we can do!" He further added and this time with an air of excitement in his words.

"What?" I replied with equal exuberance. "We can hit Harold up for some money to get a hamburger or something." Kenny was now grinning from ear to ear as he made the final comment. It didn't take us long to realize that our older sibling was not in the building, so we decided to try the fellowship hall next door.

The fellowship hall was directly across a little two-lane road. It was there that Carl's daughter Donna had fallen down and was covered by large water roaches when the pastor first showed us the complex the night before. She ran into the building the moment the doors were opened and had fallen on the hardwood floors before a light could be switched on. There must have been roaches already huddled in the darkness when she tripped, because several of them ran over her at once while she laid there on the floor. She screamed loudly to say the least and it seemed to take forever to calm her down.

Kenny noticed that the door was unlocked as we stepped up onto the small porch. Without saying a word, he turned the knob and we stepped inside. As our eyes adjusted to the darkness of the musty smelling dark paneled fellowship hall, we could see several long folding tables and plenty of metal folding chairs propped against the walls on the left side. We could also hear the distinct sound of someone heaving, a sound that apparently was echoing from the other side of the large room.

"Look there!" Kenny said abruptly, while pointing his left index finger in the direction of someone standing over the kitchen sink. "Come on," he said with a smirk. Within just a few short steps of where we had been standing, it was clear to see that the individual who was making the horrible wrenching sounds was none other than Harold himself.

When we finally arrived at the kitchen sink, Harold was splashing water on his face as he dry heaved into the basin. Setting beside him on the right counter was a half-pint carton of half-and-half milk. We knew that Harold had an ulcer at the time and that he only drank the nasty concoction whenever it was acting up. The strange thing about it was that there was a half-finished vanilla milkshake on the counter as well. "Are you sick or something?" Kenny questioned, as he lifted the milk carton up and held it closer to his face in order to read its label. All Harold could do was nod his head and heave again. "Do you think you've got the flu?" Kenny inquired, with all the inquisitiveness of a doctor analyzing a patient.

Harold splashed more water on his face and this time on the back of his neck as well. "What's this?" Kenny asked, with a tone of curiosity in his voice, as he picked up the milkshake and began to examine its contents as if he was some kind of an understudy to Sherlock Holmes.

"Ooh!" Kenny bellowed, as he jerked his head back quickly from the gross appearance of a foreign substance within its content. "There's half a roach in this milkshake!" He further announced. Harold heaved a third time and a fourth before splashing more water on his face and neck. "Well!" Kenny declared as if he had just solved the world's greatest mystery. "If there's only half of the roach in this glass, then you must have eaten the other half!" And with that statement, Harold nearly heaved his toes up.

"Well!" Kenny said in a voice that had suddenly switched from curious to sarcastic humor. "So, you snuck off to get a milkshake, did you?" His words were now being purposely slurred, in order to allow him plenty of latitude with his intended target. "Got sick for not including your little brothers right?" Harold was in no mood to laugh, but immediately recognized Kenny's words of correction, veiled in satirism. Kenny cocked his left eyebrow and gazed down at the back of Harold's head as if he were staring down the barrel of a gun attempting to get a bead on something to shoot. "Seems to me," he continued with an air of sarcasm in his tone, "God's judging someone. Must be for refusing to buy his hungry brothers a milkshake." Kenny's tenor was obviously humorous, but Harold was growing more frustrated by the second. He kept trying to speak quickly between heaves.

"Leave me alone now! I mean it!" As we were walking towards the entrance of the hall, Harold added one extra comment. "I don't care if I ever see another milk shake in my life!"

As we stepped out of the fellowship hall into the bright sunlight, Kenny started laughing. "You know what would be cool?" Kenny suggested while chuckling between words. "When Harold gets on the bus tonight, we should all have a milk shake in our hands."

That night, we had another powerful singing at one of the local churches in the Houston area. But when we got back to the facility where we had been staying, we immediately encountered that same heaviness that we had felt the previous evening when the noises first started. Coming back up stairs that night after brushing our teeth and using the restroom, we had just closed the upstairs door behind us when Kenny turned to observe light shining through the little glass square window, which clearly indicated someone had forgot to turn the light off. "Didn't I turn that light off down stairs and didn't we walk up here in the dark?" Kenny asked with an obvious confusion in his tone. Both Jerry and I agreed that we thought he turned it off and yet we were back in a giggling mode and neither one of us could be certain.

Kenny asked us to follow him back down stairs to witness his action of flicking the switch off. As soon as we had climbed the stairs and were about to enter a second time, the light came on again! "Oh, man!" Kenny blurted out suddenly. In unison, the three of us ran through the door and down to Harold's room. We were still knocking on Harold's door, when the commotion began down in the sanctuary again. "Harold!" Kenny shouted at the door, "open up man!" Kenny's voice sounded desperate.

Harold opened the door and informed us that he thought the events going on were demons there to torment us. Simultaneously, Yvonne had been experiencing a premonition that someone was looking into her bedroom window from the adjacent building. She felt that something very evil was going to take place if we did not gather for prayer to ask for God's protection! Carl and his family had became so unnerved by the strange noises and Yvonne's bad feeling, that they moved up stairs into the room next to Ronny's.

Harold decided to call a meeting to discuss what all the strange events were about, as most of the group had already heard the noises for themselves. So the entire group came together in the outer room on the upper level. With

Harold sitting on a chair facing the rest of us who were sitting in the pews, we discussed everything that had happened and who or what we thought it was. No sooner had we begun to convey our feelings and opinions, than Harold threw his arms straight out into the air, the palms of his hands facing down. He called for silence in the room. "Shush," he whispered. Harold pointed his left index finger straight up toward the large intake vents directly overhead. These were not normal size intake vents--these were massive by anyone's standards. Nonetheless, Harold thought he heard someone talking from inside the one above us. "That's it!" Harold abruptly announced, as he quickly stood to his feet and shoved the chair to one side. "All you guys come with me." Harold now seemed to be taking command of the entire situation, whether we liked it or not. "We're going down stairs and looking in everyplace there is to look," he added. "If there is anybody down there, we're gonna find 'em." He emphasized his final statement by shaking his doubled up fist and nodding his head.

Without another word, every male in the upper quarters stampeded down the flight of stairs, while Yvonne, Mary, Nancy, Donna, Ronny Junior, barricaded themselves inside Ronny's room. We rushed down the stairs that second time even more fiercely than the first time. Like a band of wild Comanche Indians, we screamed and hollered to the top of our lungs, dashing from one door to the next in the down stairs corridor. There were at least as many Sunday school classrooms downstairs as up. Any number of tormentors could be hiding inside one of them, hoping to go completely undetected. However, if they were here, we would find them. That was of course, providing that they were humans and not demons as Harold suspected.

After a thorough investigation of every nook and cranny, we finally decided that Harold might be right about the demons. We all concluded that Yvonne's feelings were correct and we needed to pray quickly.

We gathered into the sanctuary for prayer and as tradition would have it, we knelt at the altar to do so. All of a sudden, without prior arrangement, each of us turned in an almost synchronized fashion and looked over our shoulders towards the port-holed doors dividing the auditorium from the foyer I had investigated earlier. Each one of us felt as if we were being observed through the glass of those portholes. It literally seemed like someone had poured cold ice water over our heads. One by one, we jumped to our feet and ran out of the sanctuary and back to the safety of the upstairs classrooms.

Harold took it one step further and grabbed his mattress up and went to the bus. If Harold was going, so were Kenny and I. It was a steam bath out there, but it did feel safe and serene. Kenny and I sweated profusely and were completely drained of energy the next day. No one else had slept either; we were all too busy being afraid.

When we finally came back from our third night of engagements in Houston, Kenny and I decided to try the classroom again. Harold was not coming back in under any circumstances. Yvonne still felt like she was being watched and asked if we would sleep outside her door for safety reasons. Jerry, Kenny and I all placed our mattresses on the floor directly in front of the old upright piano. I personally pushed the foot of my mattress up against Yvonne's door, seeing that it opened out into the hall and someone would have to move me to get to her. Kenny slept in the middle next to me, with Jerry on the far side.

As we lay on our stomachs, we could look straight under the rows of benches and see the windowed door clearly. We could also see that the light we had turned off coming to bed was back on. The three of us lay there in the shadowy darkness with only the faint light from a street lamp shining through the large bay window at the other end of the room next to the door we were eyeing. "Don't go to sleep guys!" Kenny muttered as he rested his chin on the back of his overlapped hands. "Whatever you do, we must stay awake until dawn." Kenny was of the mind set that like ghosts, vampires or any other creature of the night, demons could not torment people in the daylight. I don't know where he got that concept from, but it seemed logical to us at the time. The one thing that truly seemed to bother Kenny and me was that we were sleeping directly below the same vent that Harold had heard the voices coming from earlier.

"They're probably watching us right now," Kenny mumbled. The thought of that nearly freaked me out and I couldn't help casting a leery eye in the direction of the intake vent. Every time we thought we heard someone coming up the stairs, the air conditioner would kick on. When we thought we heard talking in the vent, the air would start up again. Before long, Jerry was snoring, and when Kenny looked over to observe Jerry's position, he noticed that Jerry slept with the whites of his eyes showing. This really bothered Kenny. He leaned over and whispered in my ear. "Larry?"

"Yeah?" I responded in a cracking voice.

"Look at Jerry's eyes. Do you see that?" Kenny's tone indicated near panic.

"Oh, my God!" I said at a volume level loud enough to have wakened the average person, but Jerry never moved.

Kenny whispered even softer now. "Larry, he looks devil possessed." Kenny's eyes were so wide and frightened; he was really starting to scare me! "Come to think of it," Kenny added, "we didn't have any problems like this until he joined the group."

Somehow, I couldn't imagine someone being used of God under the anointing of the Holy Spirit and being devil possessed at the same time. But I wasn't certain about those things back then. Yet I knew one thing: The problems we were experiencing weren't happening with us in here where Jerry was, but out there where Jerry wasn't. "I don't think he's possessed, Kenny. If he was, he would have been frothing at the mouth or something a long time ago." It may not have been the most theological answer, but it seemed to appease Kenny for the moment.

After an hour or so of vigilant watching, I began to lose consciousness. Kenny remained on watch until the first streams of sunlight began to penetrate into the dark room. Feeling that the necessity to remain awake had now finally passed, Kenny slipped off into a deep and long awaited slumber.

According to Kenny's later report, he fell asleep somewhere around 5:30 in the morning. I woke about 6:30, almost one hour exactly from the time he closed his eyes to sleep. To my dismay, the heavy windowed door at the end of the upstairs auditorium stood completely open. I reached for Kenny instinctively and shook him awake. "Kenny!" I said in a trembling voice. "Look at the door, it's standing wide open." Kenny didn't need to stop and rub the sleep from his swollen eyes. Adrenaline immediately rushed through his body at such a rapid pace that he sat straight up and turned to observe the strange phenomenon. Next, he slowly turned and looked directly into my eyes, with his own eyes nearly bugging out of his head.

"This is crazy, man," Kenny announced. "Whoever or whatever it was, it was standing right over us while we slept. We've got find out if anyone has come in or gone out that door and might have left it standing open while we were asleep," he declared, as if he were about to begin a police investigation to catch a murderer. However, after questioning everyone in the building, even Harold, who had spent a second night in the bus, we finally concluded that no one had been through the door since we initially closed it the night before. That would definitely confirm some sort of outside entity attempting to frighten and maybe even harm us, if Yvonne's feelings were correct.

When nightfall came and we had finished our evening's engagement, none of us wanted to go back to what some of us were calling "the haunted church." Yet, with no money and nowhere else to stay but the hot bus, we reluctantly returned for another long night. However, we decided that evening that enough was enough and that we had allowed the devil to push around too long. We decided to have a serious prayer meeting right there in the upstairs annex. We prayed diligently, commanding every demonic force of Satan to leave by the blood of Jesus Christ.

Believe it or not, we never had one other single disturbing experience, during the remainder of our stay that week. Later on, as we prepared to leave town, the pastor informed us of his main reason for inviting us to stay at his church. According to what he told us, he had brought us there to test whether or not we would experience strange events like he had experienced in the past. Upon hearing this little tidbit of information, Kenny looked over at me from his seat on the bus and said, "Why couldn't he just cast out his own devils, instead of having to have us do it for him?"

Many years later, my wife and I went to visit Kenny in Houston where he was the pastor of his own church. While sitting at his dinning room table one night, he decided to drive the two of us out to the old haunted church on Zoo Street. As we pulled into the parking lot of the place of our childhood fears, Kenny laughed and asked me, "Could you spend the night in the old place if you had to, Larry?" His tone was neither sarcastic nor humorous. It seemed almost anointed as he spoke that evening in 1990 behind the wheel of his Lincoln Continental.

"Yeah, Kenny," I said slapping my hands against my knees and glancing his way with a grin on my face. " I believe I can do all things through Christ which strengthens me!"

Kenny just chuckled and said, "Amen! Larry, the devil knew that God had a plan for our lives, so he started very early on to discourage us from ever reaching our goal." Kenny's voice was strong and assertive, as if he were on the verge of preaching a sermon. He continued to speak with his right index finger poking the air to emphasize his statements. "The devil knew God was going to use us to touch lives all over the world and although we didn't always manage to follow God like we should have, God knew His plan would ultimately prevail and we would come through successfully!" When we drove away that final time from the place of our early testing, I knew in my heart that Kenny was right and that it all made perfect sense.

    If the devil can frighten you in any fashion that will cause you to go home defeated and overwhelmed with failure, he will have succeeded in preventing your destiny and stopping your ministry. If, on the other hand, you take authority over your fears and cast the enemy out of your life, he has no choice but to watch you go on with the purpose God has determined for you. (Jeremiah 29:11.)

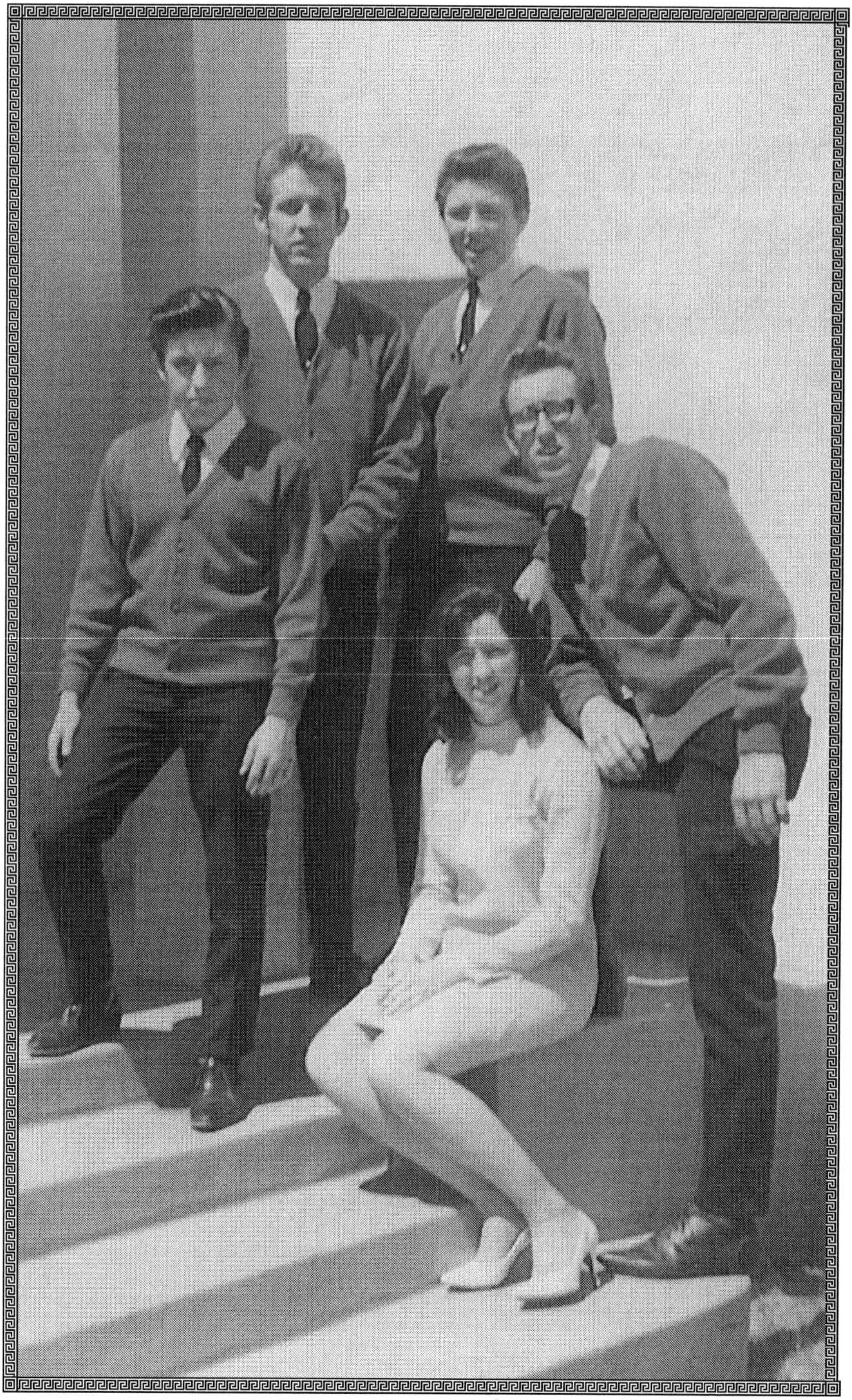

# CHAPTER SEVEN

## A TASTE OF THE BIG TIME

During one of our many family rehearsals at the Pentecostal Tabernacle in Salinas, we caught a glimpse into the future of a legend. Up until that time, we had recorded two projects, which consisted mostly of other people's material. Ronny sang the lead on both of these projects. This forced our harmony arrangements into a rather weird concoction, and often one us, if not all of us, were driven right out of our individual ranges. Nothing seemed to quite gel.

It was easy enough for me to sing a soprano position when I was still eleven and twelve years old, however, turning thirteen changed everything for me. That night at the Tabernacle, after enduring a long strenuous practice session and struggling with the frustration of once more performing second hand material, our focus and energy started to wane. It was nearly two o'clock in the morning and we had worked all night on just a handful of songs. Nothing was working out and most of us were ready to call it quits for the night. As the session seemed to be winding down and the general consensus was one of a wasted evening, everyone started to slowly disperse. Yvonne went out to the lobby and got a drink from the drinking fountain and started reading some church literature in the foyer. I went up to the balcony for an overview and sat down. Ronny went to the restroom downstairs. Carl put down his bass and stood up to stretch, then yawned and looked at his watch. He made a comment about how late it was and how his wife would no doubt be worried about him by now.

Kenny sat on the top of his Vox amplifier, dangling his left foot, while his right foot, which was fully extended to the floor, supported his weight. His eyes glazed over and locked onto the first row of the auditorium's seats. Kenny still held his Vox guitar firmly in his hands as the strap tugged heavily against his neck and shoulders. You would have thought he was in a trance, had it not been for the repetitious motion of fingers as he picked out intricate patterns on the strings. In reality, Kenny was lost in deep meditation about something.

It seemed all too apparent that we were in a make it or break it situation and something had to give. If we were bored with our repertoire and if we felt our career was going nowhere, surely an audience would sense it as well. By now, we were already becoming known as the west coast's number one group, but we knew that the rut we were stuck in could very easily jeopardize all that. After an extensive amount of waiting, and plenty of grumbling from both Carl and Yvonne, Ronny finally emerged from the men's room downstairs. He was carrying a long sheet of toilet tissue in his hand and it fluttered in the wind behind him, as he walked in the direction of the stage. "Hey, everybody!" Ronny shouted as he stepped up onto the platform. Kenny looked up out of his intense stare and gazed at the lengthy pieces of tissue flapping behind Ronny with a curious expression. Ronny started gathering us in around him, much a like a football coach gathers in his team for some strategic advice.

"Guys," Ronny began, and although we felt somewhat like we were his players and he was ready to give us a pep talk, we stopped long enough to hear what he had to say. "I know everybody's tired and everybody wants to go home, but I think I have a good song here." The dread became immediately apparent on Carl's face and Yvonne furled her eyebrows. Kenny squinted his eyes and took on the appearance of someone concentrating hard at trying to solve a mystery. Ronny went on defending his reason for needing our cooperation so late in the game. "I believe everybody needs to just slow down and hear this song and let's see what we can do with it." Kenny was obviously as worn out as the rest of us, however, he was no doubt even more tired of the kind of material we had been doing lately. Kenny strummed his guitar strings in a familiar range to Ronny's voice. Sluggishly, everyone returned to the platform. Still in my lofty perch above the lower auditorium, I could see that everyone walked as though they were on a forced death march.

Ronny began singing the first verse of his latest composition, while each of us took our places at the microphones. As Ronny continued singing his voice seemed pleasant enough, but the words of the song really caught our attention. Yet, even as we enjoyed listening to the content of the composition the structure of the song felt more like something that a quartet might perform, rather than a mixed group. We were desperate for some new material, but we needed something with more of a family sound that would truly fit our personality.

Ronny had written some excellent words about a powerful subject. However, the song still left much to be desired. After another thirty minutes of Ronny singing the lead vocals and us attempting to harmonize, Kenny just suddenly stopped playing. "Something's not right," he muttered, lightly tapping the knuckle of his right index finger against the bottom row of his front teeth.

"Something's missing, isn't it?" Ronny asked sincerely. Kenny just nodded his head and suddenly slipped into the kind of lost expression, he had been displaying the entire time Ronny had been down stairs in the men's room writing. Ronny, tireless in his efforts to keep adjusting the tune and readjusting the phrasing, attempted to find a workable solution. Workable, however, was what we had already been singing, so the last thing we needed right now was something workable. Eventually, Ronny felt as though he was losing the battle as well as the interest of the group and surrendered to the overall dampened mood that saturated the practice session.

Ronny took the long roll of bathroom tissue, wadded it up and tossed it into the little waste paper basket near the pulpit. Then he literally threw both hands into the air, and smacked his palms against either of his legs, as he let them free fall to his sides. He could not imagine that all his hard work had been to no avail. For a few more minutes, Kenny continued to say nothing, as he seemed to remain oblivious to his current surroundings. He just kept playing a variety of short, fast licks on the guitar.

Ronny had already left the stage and was starting to mill around like someone who was not sure of his or her direction, when all at once Kenny blurted out, "Let me see something." Then in one fluent motion, he stepped forward, stretched out his arm and wrapped his fingers about the crumpled lyric sheet resting in the tiny trash receptacle. Next, he carefully placed it on the top of the podium and smoothed out its surface with the palm of his hands. Once he managed to press enough wrinkles from the tissue to see the words clearly, he spoke out with a confidence in his tone. "Let me try this," he said, as he strummed a chord on the strings of his guitar and started singing the song from an entirely different perspective.

"There's a lighthouse on the hillside and it overlooks life's sea." This time, the words had the unique resemblance to something directly from the country music charts.

As Kenny continued to sing the first verse, shock waves seemed to pulsate throughout the entire sanctuary. The same lyrics, that only a few minutes ago seemed to lack a significant direction or flavor, now carried a totally new expression! Kenny sang with a down home country slur to his words, that seemed to fit the song perfectly.

"Move over Merle Haggard," I said at a volume loud enough for all to hear. Ronny displayed a crooked smirk and Yvonne nodded her head in approval smiling from ear to ear, as she turned her eyes to meet mine. Carl wore a broad grin across his face, as he attempted to follow along with the slightly altered melody on his bass guitar. No one felt as tired and sleepy as they had minutes ago! Instead, we stood in amazement watching the lone artist standing in front of the microphone. Kenny had never expressed this much country overtone in any other song we had sang or recorded to date.

The longer Kenny sang, the wider Ronny's mouth gaped. Ronny knew it, and so did we: this was the right formula. Not just the right ingredient for a great song, but the right ingredient for a powerful identity in southern gospel music for the group as a whole.

Although no one present that night had the courage to admit it, all of us knew deep down inside that the song was definitely a hit!

That night a disaster was averted and a miracle transpired. A legend was being molded and a masterpiece was being shaped. "The Singer," as Kenny would later come to be called, was preparing to take his rightful place in the annals of gospel music history. The Hinson Family would ultimately go on to record "The Lighthouse" on their very next project by the same name. In addition, because of Kenny's unusual display of vocal ability that night and because it gave us a more unified harmony, we decided that he should take the lead position on almost all of our future songs.

Night after night, on stage after stage, audiences up and down the west coast thrilled to the newly demonstrated vocal talents of Kenny Hinson singing "The Lighthouse." Kenny seemed to excel in a fashion far exceeding anything that any of us had expected. Many were the times that I felt more like a backup singer than someone worthy of sharing the same spotlight with him. Kenny pioneered a sound in professional southern gospel music that did not exist prior to his arrival on the scene. And while none of us could have possibly realized it at the time, he was actually blazing a trail for country gospel and Christian country artists to follow for years to come! While Kenny would eventually prove himself versatile enough to sing virtually any style of song with any number of characteristics added to it, country gospel just felt natural to him. Fans, promoters, pastors and DJs alike, found Kenny's "Merle Haggard" flavor capable of filling a void that the gospel music of that day somehow lacked for them. Now, instead of abandoning their music style of choice, these individuals could put their 8-track of Kenny Hinson into their player and hear about God rather than "cheating hearts or crying in my beer."

Even Rusty Goodman of The Happy Goodman Family wanted to sing and record the song after hearing Kenny's rendition. This is when we initially went to record our Lighthouse project at Goodman Sound Studios in Madisonville, Kentucky. In 1971, the Happy Goodman Family was one of the co-hosts of the nationally acclaimed "Gospel Singing Jubilee." This television program aired all over the United States, and anyone who claimed to be a Christian, regardless of race or background, seemed to watch its Sunday morning concerts faithfully.

The Goodmans had been greatly impressed by the song "The Lighthouse" and wanted us to be their guest on the program. Jubilee's main host Les Beasley of The Florida Boys, allowed us to present the song on the show, which later aided it in winning the Favorite Song of the Year award at The Singing News Fan Awards that same year.

Once Les Beasley agreed to our appearance on the show we packed up and climbed into a very cramped 1970 Buick La Sabre and headed off for Nashville, Tennessee. We were extremely excited about having the opportunity to perform on the program. It really didn't seem to matter that we weren't exactly going to arrive in style. The only thing that seemed important at the time was that we had a shot at the big time. Dragging along behind the bright red Buick was a U-haul trailer with our clothes and equipment in it.

I can't remember if our bus was broken down at the time or if we had simply sold it, however, we had to make the best of things. Although it was extremely hot, Kenny and I took our turn riding in the trailer pulled behind the car. We were very excited about being in Nashville, yet we were tremendously nervous as well. In the summer of 1971, Kenny was only seventeen and I had not yet turned fifteen. We felt we had entered a world of Gospel music giants when we finally arrived at the television studio.

They introduced us and Kenny stepped to the microphone to sing "The Lighthouse." We could all see how truly scared he was. Under the hot camera lights, he wore a thick coat of pancake makeup, which had been applied liberally by the make up artist in the dressing room. The orange tinted powder stained his shirt all around the collar. The makeup also seemed to amplify all of the nervousness on his face as he began singing the first words of the song.

I wondered just how nervous I looked to those watching us perform. Recently, I received the answer to my question as I had the pleasure of viewing some re-released videos of the occasion. While watching Bill Gaither's "The Jubilee Years featuring The Hinsons" in a two-volume set, I laughed till I cried. There is absolutely no doubt that we appeared frightened out of our minds to the viewing audience. You can certainly watch our confidence increase as the years of filming the show dramatically prove throughout the rest of the tapes. However, watching that particular segment brought back the feelings and the memories we both experienced that first day of filming.

Kenny desperately attempted to mask his fear of the dark glass ominous eye staring back at him, just seconds before its red light popped on to inform him that the nation was watching through its lens. When it was over, Kenny confided in me privately, "I was shaking like a leaf! I hope no one could tell."

"I know," I said in an anxious tenor. "I was scared to death, too!" We had all become accustomed to following

# A TASTE OF THE BIG TIME

Kenny's directions on stage. So much in fact that while watching the Gaither video, I couldn't help but notice how often we turned to watch what he was going to do next.

Little did we know when we returned to California that summer that we had become television stars overnight to many people as a result of that appearance on Jubilee! I remember wondering back then how different our lives would become since we had filmed such a major gospel music television show.

"Ladies and Gentlemen, please make welcome the west coast's number one gospel group, The Singing Hinson Family!" That's the way we were introduced after that, and the master of ceremonies would go on to inform the audience of our recent guest appearance on "The Gospel Singing Jubilee." Although we were still quite young and new to the gospel music industry, I fully expected the kind of hardships we had already endured to soon become just a memory. I was certain that this was the change we'd been waiting for and working for so long. Traveling up and down the highways, in bus that spent more time broken down than it did getting us to each engagement would soon be a thing of the past, I thought. Perhaps we would be able to afford a newer, more glamorous coach. It somehow seems difficult to feel glamorous or successful about your career when the sweltering summer heat keeps reminding you that your current coach has no working air conditioner. And yet we kept dreaming of a brighter tomorrow!

We were already beginning to rub shoulders with more of the major groups and plans were currently underway for a tour in the East. The Goodmans had invited us to move to Madisonville, Kentucky where Sam Goodman was supposedly going to help us book some engagements. That same year, we were able to purchase a 1960 Silver Eagle, a used bus from the Continental Trailways Bus Company.

"The Lighthouse" had been voted the number one song of the year by The Singing News Fan Awards and we felt as though we were crowding the professional market rapidly.

That summer, in 1971, Kenny and I decided to start using some of this newfound popularity to our advantage. That is of course, where girls were concerned. Kenny and I were beginning to discover that being a celebrity had its benefits. We found out quickly that the pretty girls, usually snobbish and unwilling to give us the time of day, fell all over themselves when we came around due to our recently acquired fame. Flirtations flowed freely from both sides and our egos received a temporary inflation. These girls could not possibly picture us sweating in our broken down bus along the side of the road. Nor could they imagine us as eight people crammed into one car traveling almost two thousand miles to film the Jubilee. These young ladies only saw one thing when the Hinsons came to town: "Stars!"

Kenny and I sort of entered into a competition with regard to celebrity status. The competition really consisted of which one of us could get the most girl friends. Cute girls were worth more points! However, as long as they were decent, they counted as a point. Of course, we did have a rule between us competitors that you had to prove that someone was in fact your girlfriend through the evidence of regular correspondence. This private competition would extend for the next three or four years and by 1974, I was personally writing over twenty different girls each month. The truth is, that the need for fresh blood (so to speak) became so bad, that some band members actually had to inform us of whom they liked in order to prevent Kenny and I from staking our own claims. We finally had to enter into an agreement with them, promising not to attempt to steal their girl friends from them. Of course we honored the agreement, although in our youthful arrogance we both believed we could have stolen them at any given time.

Kenny and I started flexing our muscles when it came to the opposite sex. At the time, we changed girl friends nearly as frequently as we changed shirts. Kenny was even more fickle about relationships with the female gender than I was. He could be totally crazy about a girl one week and be completely disinterested the next.

I only knew of one girl in those earliest days that Kenny was really fond of. She lived in the town of Salinas where we were based. She had broken Kenny's young heart and he would revert into a quite sullen mood when her name was even brought up. He simply wouldn't talk about it, no matter how I attempted to discuss her with him. Maybe the relationship had damaged him badly enough that he was simply distrusting of any relationships. For this reason, I believe he always bailed out first before the young lady had even the slightest chance of losing interest in him. This of course, was no less than an emotional protection mechanism. By nature, Kenny was a real pacifist, a non-confrontationalist, to say the least, and his method of breaking off a relationship could often appear cold and evasive.

I, on the other hand, had far too bold a personality to avoid a confrontation if necessary. However, I was also more conservative when it came to relationships and enjoyed the security of knowing that the same person would pretty much be there for me whenever I came to their city or town. While I often had a difficult time keeping up with the names of Kenny's newest girl friends, after a while Kenny came to recognize some of my female companions rather well. Ronny of course, was always complaining about Kenny and I leaving the wrong impression with the Christian crowd, pastors and concert promoters. He felt we were being far too affectionate in public, by holding hands with our girlfriends or having our arms around them at our singings. Kenny and I always joked with one another in private about Ronny preferring us to walk the corridors of the concert halls and churches wearing large crosses about our necks and holding huge family Bibles in our hands. This would adequately display our sincerity to the masses.

In most cases, we did our very best to provide some level of damage control, but in some situations, that was nearly impossible to do. Especially when you felt you had a particularly pretty girl hanging on your arm. Sometimes it just seemed necessary to show that girl off at the record table during intermission. I was always attracted to more assertive personalities than shy ones. Sometimes, however, assertive turned into demanding and such was the occasion that took place that summer of 1971.

You see, sometimes these girlfriends would find out that they were not the only individuals we were seeing, and they could grow rather jealous from time to time. A few of them even became somewhat violent. Those kinds of relationships can really take their toll on your emotions.

I once spent most of the night in the men's room at the National Quartet Convention hiding from five different girlfriends of mine who decided to show up for the event on the same evening. I couldn't afford to run the risk of their open display of anger right in the midst of the biggest gospel music event of the year. Needless to say, I barely got out of the building that night with my life. Thank God, Kenny eventually walked into the bathroom and agreed to run some diversionary tactics for me.

One evening in Turlock, California caused me to clearly realize the consequences of a jealous confrontation and I was not eager to repeat that encounter in Nashville, where the convention was being held at the time. Turlock was still a sore spot for me and Kenny almost never let me live it down.

The summer of 1971 went extremely well, until my girlfriend Terry found out about another girl I was with in the town of Modesto. She managed to embarrass me in front of a few fans at the Turlock High School Auditorium one night, demanding exclusiveness or else! Her ranting and raving only served to humiliate me and so I immediately started planning for my revenge. Kenny of course, didn't help matters any when he heard the loud commotion and started laughing and shaking his head at me. You talk about adding insult to injury. There was no doubt in my mind that he thought I couldn't control my relationships. Needless to say, this would not happen again at least as far as I was concerned. A little later, while riding the bus back to Salinas, Kenny looked at me and asked me a question. "You're not going to take it off that girl, are you?"

"Of course not!" I snapped back. "She's a nut and she's gonna pay!" I quickly added. Kenny cast a gaze in my direction indicating his disbelief.

"We'll see," he replied sarcastically.

Boy, was my manhood ever offended that night! I had to figure out a way to save face. After all, no one treated someone of my gospel music status that way and got away with it. I knew that we would be returning to Turlock in just a couple of months, so I had to get my revenge organized quickly. My wounded pride required a form of revenge that would not allow her to retaliate. After several days of deliberation, I finally settled on a plan. It was just diabolical enough to prove to Kenny that I wouldn't be pushed around by some hotheaded girl.

A few days after arriving back home from Turlock, I received a letter from Terry wherein she preceded to read me the riot act. I became more determined than ever to let her have it good. So I wrote her a letter to leave the impression that I was cowing down to her demands. When Kenny realized that we were headed right back to Turlock in just a few weeks, he asked me flatly, "Do have everything under control with this Terry girl?"

"I sure do!" I replied with all the confidence of one who was able to predict the future. "She's gonna pay all right," I added.

"Well, you'd better take care this matter before it causes you a problem with Ronny," Kenny now warned soberly.

"I will. It's gonna be just fine, you wait and see," I retorted in frustration. I wrote Terry to ask her to join me at the upcoming concert in Turlock. Terry was already fully aware of the fact that Ronny didn't want any of the frontline in the group to be seen by the crowd until they walked onto the stage for the first time in any given concert. She was also aware that Ronny frowned upon girls being back stage at a concert, since it might not sit well with the concert promoter. Kenny and I referenced the back stage area as the "No fan zone."

For this reason, I wrote Terry and requested she rendezvous with me at the record table during intermission. In addition, I wrote my girlfriend Doris in Modesto and asked if she would be able to drive over to join me for the concert that evening. I asked her to meet me at the back stage entrance of the high school.

After executing this plan, I ran into a world of unexpected trouble. Initially, everything came down without a hitch. According to one of our band members, Terry was in the correct place, right at the time of intermission. Doris was back stage with me when it was time for the group to head to the record table. Ronny didn't like her being there one bit, but the promoter didn't seem to mind and it was worth the chewing out I'd no doubt get later in order to see Terry get what was coming to her.

I felt pretty good about my plan on the way up to Turlock as I lay in my private bunk aboard our Silver Eagle bus still painted the Continental Trailways colors of pale yellow with a large z shaped stripe down either side. Kenny had asked me one final time during the trip up there if I was going to be seeing Terry and if I had everything under control. I had assured him that everything was quite in hand. Now that I was only moments away from executing my plan, I was really quite eager to watch Terry eat crow!

As I walked with Doris along the hallway leading down the left side of the auditorium, I knew that I was only seconds away from revenge. Soon we would round the corner at the end of the hallway and emerge into the large lobby area where our record table was set up and Terry would be waiting to join me. Boy, was she going to get the shock of her life and no doubt beg my forgiveness once she saw how striking Doris was! Kenny was directly behind us as we stepped into the lobby and all at once he stepped up on my right side and whispered in my ear, "I hope you know what you're doing!" I waved my right hand in a gesture of complete confidence as we continued in a straight line for the table.

People were packed into the lobby like toothpicks inside a box. There was a small clearing between another local group's table and ours, so I nearly drug Doris through the opening in order to get behind our table. All at once I looked up to see Terry standing directly in front of the table where she had been talking to Yvonne while awaiting my arrival. Immediately the smile on her face melted into anger. Her eyes suddenly darted from me to the dark headed young lady holding my hand only a couple of feet away.

Without warning, the blonde hothead dropped a hydrogen bomb right in the middle of the lobby of the Turlock High School auditorium. She started stomping her feet rapidly like a little kid throwing a tantrum. The scream reminded of something you might see on one of those late night B-rated Chinese movies, when two fighters engage in battle. She started shaking her fist at me and calling me every conceivable name one could call someone without using a curse word of some sort. Needless to say, everyone immediately stopped talking and laughing and purchasing records.

Now it appeared that every eye was on Terry and me. You talk about feeling humiliated! I felt so low down that I could have easily hid in my socks. Terry was throwing what Mama would have classified as an old fashioned "Hissy fit." Evidently, my fail-safe plan had failed. I had certainly expected a negative reaction, but never to this extent. Not to mention the fact that things weren't looking too hopeful with regard to her begging for my forgiveness either. My vision of exacting some revenge for our former encounter had altogether backfired and now obviously I was looking pretty stupid in the eyes of the entire concert crowd.

Just when I was certain that I had reached the pinnacle of humiliation, I felt a firm hand from behind as someone grasped my right collarbone and squeezed it tightly. I instantly recognized the wristwatch and knew it was Kenny. As I slowly made the agonizing turn to meet his gaze, he dropped his head and leaned into my left ear to whisper, "The plan?" He continued with a chuckle in his voice. "Do you by any chance have another one, because I don't think this one's working!" Embarrassment gave way to anger at the sarcastic overtones of Kenny's remarks. "Have fun explaining this to Ronny!" Kenny added, as he retreated back into the mob of spectators now filling the gap where he'd just been standing, the same way that water reclaims the sandy footprints left by someone walking along the sea shore. I waved my hand at Terry as if to indicate I'd heard enough and quickly pushed my way through the mass of people.

I held fast to Doris' hand as I made my way to the back stage area again. Ronny would no doubt be climbing my case before the night was over, I thought. No explanation was going to be good enough, that much I knew for sure. I was never going to hear the last of this one and it could very well bring a halt to inviting girlfriends to concerts all together! When I reached the backstage area with Doris, Kenny looked at me and started laughing. Poor Doris still hadn't said a word. She was probably in shock and no doubt just as embarrassed as I was. She'll never come to see me again, I thought to myself. She's gotta think I am crazy for setting all this up.

I did my very best to give Doris a clear and precise explanation about how the entire ordeal transpired and finally convinced her that I had already decided to be finished with Terry long before the evening started. Kenny kept shaking his head and laughing at me from the wings of the curtains on the other side of the backstage area.

That night on the bus, Ronny informed me of the irreparable damage I had created with regard to our ever having another invitation to sing anywhere in the United

States. This night's little escapade literally took me a couple of years to live down. For the longest time, Kenny would come up to me somewhere and say, "I have a girlfriend coming to the concert this week that I really don't want to be with. Do you have any suggestions about how I could get rid of her privately and quietly?" He'd raise his eyebrows at the conclusion of his satirical question and cast me a look that clearly identified his sarcasm.

Oh! How many times I would have loved to have grabbed a piece of a brick, if only I could have found one lying around somewhere!

# CHAPTER EIGHT

## THE BIG MOVE

By 1971, The Hinson's were pretty much a household name on the west coast. We were even starting to get dates as far south as the Los Angeles area. Remember, this was at a time in America when contemporary Christian music was still in its infancy. Southern gospel music, however, dominated the playing field and we were jumping right into the middle of it with both feet. We were very excited about the transition from California to Kentucky since we were just really starting to break into areas where promoters like Poly Grimes controlled the talent.

We were eager to spread our wings in the lower half of the Golden State as well. When October of that year rolled around, we had some dates scheduled in and around Los Angeles. It was during this particular month that we sang at a little Pentecostal Holiness church in Ontario, California.

The pastor, Reverend Jessie Cluck, showed Ronny and our new bass player Rick Howeth where the electrical outlets were on the stage for our sound equipment and amplifiers. I assisted the rest of the guys in the group carrying in the stage equipment. Then I turned my attention to setting up our record table items. Kenny helped bring in the three projects we had available at that time. After helping me get set up, he returned to the platform and began to set up his guitar and amplifier, as I worked diligently for the next few

# THE BIG MOVE

moments getting everything properly arranged for public display. Due to the small space allotted for us to place our table and record racks, I had chosen to position them directly against the opposite wall from the platform, next to the entrance door of the small sanctuary. After I had finished placing everything in order, I took one giant step back and surveyed the table for anything that was out of place or missing.

As I stepped forward again to straighten the 8 x 10 glossy pictures of the group that we offered for sale, I noticed a small prayer box attached to and protruding from the back wall. It was complete with a miniature door that you could open in order to collect the prayer requests. Someone had scotch taped a hand written sign to the top of the box that read "Open in case of fire!" I couldn't resist. Curiosity got the best of me and no sooner had I opened the tiny receptacle than I burst into laughter. Someone had placed a glass of water inside! "Now that's my kind of humor," I thought. Kenny was still on the stage tuning his instrument, when I called out to him to come check out the prayer box.

"Hey, Kenny!" I yelled out loudly, forgetting for a moment that there were already some people in the auditorium who had arrived early for the concert. "You gotta come see this prayer box! It's hilarious!" I chuckled, pointing my index finger in the direction of the little pinewood container.

"What is it?" Kenny replied, lifting his eyebrows and tilting his head back slightly at the same time, indicating a request for additional information.

"No!" I said, once again pointing at the small prayer box. "You're going to have to come see this for yourself." Kenny unstrapped his guitar and carefully placed it into its guitar stand before descending from the stage and trotting back to where I was standing. Kenny was old enough at this particular time to want to maintain his personal dignity in the presence of complete strangers. However this was not meant to be. "Read that sign on the box," I instructed, as I motioned in its direction, jabbing the air with my left thumb.

Kenny read it aloud and then cautiously pulled back on the wooden knob, as if he were afraid that a snake would jump out. As the tiny door swung back on its miniature hinges, Kenny started cracking up immediately. I was grinning from ear to ear, as I watched Kenny lose every ounce of self-control, as he laughed so fast and hard; it reminded me of a jackhammer pounding away at some pavement. "That's great!" Kenny exclaimed, in a voice loud enough to turn a few heads. "That's one of the funniest things I've seen in a long time!" he announced as he covered his lips with the palm of his hand. "I wonder who did it."

All at once, a female's voice could be heard in response to Kenny's question. "She did it!" One of the young girls sitting near the back of the short auditorium shouted. I looked up to see a fairly tall girl pointing a finger over the head of a shorter dark headed girl who was sitting next to her. Kenny pointed in the direction of the shorter girl. "Did you put the water there?" Kenny asked.

"I did it," the girl raised the palm of her right hand up, in a gesture of admittance.

"That's so funny!" Kenny confessed. "Where did you ever come up with an idea like that?"

The short girl replied, "I don't know. I just thought of it a few days ago during one of our services. I thought surely one of the ushers would find it and remove it before now," she went on to explain. The taller girl may have been attractive, but I really didn't notice. To me, the shorter one was incredibly beautiful and possessed a more forward personality in just the manner I preferred. The only thing was, someone that good looking would not be interested in me, that is, not with Kenny around I thought.

I was pleasantly surprised to discover that in reality, the girl was actually interested in me after all. She came to the remaining services around the vicinity and I eventually found out her name was Jana Hartley. She even gave me her

# THE BIG MOVE

address and I promised her that I would write. This girl intimidated me because of her overwhelming good looks. So much in fact, that although only two months passed before I saw her again, it was like meeting her for the first time. Although she came to the Long Beach auditorium, where we were in concert with The Goodmans, I was too shy to be around her. She walked all over the building attempting to locate me, and yet I remained somewhat aloof. Perhaps it was because I was just certain that once she really got to know me, she wouldn't actually like me. Whatever the reason, she kept asking Kenny where his little brother was.

Towards the end of the evening, I finally mustered enough courage to talk to her for a little while and squeezed her hand as she was leaving. Once again, I promised her that I would write before we moved to Kentucky. At first, Kenny asked me if my relationship with Jana was going to turn out like the one in Turlock. But by that last evening in Long Beach, he realized that my feelings for this girl were different than they had been for the other girl friends I'd had before, and he asked me if I really liked this girl a lot. I assured him that I did have much stronger feelings for Jana than the other girls, and that I hated to move now, in a way. "Did you kiss her?" he asked with a sarcastic smirk on his face.

"No!" I responded emphatically, while shaking my head back and forth from side to side. I'll never know why it was that on the one hand, I wanted my older sibling to think of me as mature and by the same token, I felt embarrassed to even act like I would consider doing anything romantic. I didn't realize that night in October of 1971 that just five years later I would walk the aisle with that same girl in holy matrimony.

Kenny and I spent the better part of that same summer working hard to get our bus ready for the permanent trip back east. There was a lot of sanding to do on the old yellow coach so that the bus could be painted gunmetal gray. Once we arrived back in Salinas, we continued to put the finishing touches on the interior of the bus. We spent a great deal of time during the winter months working in Salinas and then living with Harold over in Freedom.

Mom and Dad knew that we were going to moving into virtually unknown territory for us. They also realized that we were going to be without any place to stay, so they went ahead to rent a house for us to call home.

On March 12, 1972, we arrived to witness a snow-covered day in Madisonville, Kentucky. We were ready to get started fulfilling the long list of engagements that we were under the impression were already booked. Sam Goodman evidently found it much more difficult to schedule us back east than he had initially thought. By the time we arrived in Madisonville and called Sam, to our great disappointment, we discovered that there was not one single date scheduled except in their own church. As a result, we were in a strange land without any contacts for booking any dates.

We spent a great deal of time doing absolutely nothing but hanging around the house. Keep in mind, that our group included a full band, consisting of a bass player, drum player and piano player. For the most part, we became even closer to one another and truly began feeling like even the band members were family. Mom and Dad certainly fed them as though they were and most of the time, we even slept in the frost-covered bus along side them.

It was very difficult for Mom and Dad during those early days, seeing that they had to primarily support everyone in the group while we waited long periods of time in between dates. I guess Dad somehow anticipated the probability of having a little more difficult time than the rest of us. Being on disability pension already, his income was extremely limited and he was forced to rent a rather run down wooden house. Kenny and I were a little embarrassed initially, due to that fact that the old weather beaten home was directly across the street from Rusty Goodman, of The Happy Goodman Family. Talk about feeling humiliated! Here we were in a house that was badly in need of repair and a paint job while just across

# THE BIG MOVE

the narrow two-lane road, one of gospel music icons lived in a contemporary brick dwelling.

Yvonne did finally manage to secure a bedroom inside our house, which provided some very necessary privacy for her and us boys. We remained living in the bus well into the summer months. After a short time, our pianist Duane decided that the group was going no where fast and he was tired of freezing in the winter and burning up during the summer. Coming from a much more privileged background than any of the rest of us, we were not surprised when he packed his bags and flew home to California.

Sometime during the middle of the summer that year, for a short while we were allowed to stay in the basement of Rusty's house. Kenny really felt like we were walking in tall cotton, so to speak. That is, until shortly after we were disallowed the privilege to remain there any longer. Kenny and I always wondered if that perhaps Rusty became upset with us when Ronny decided not to sell him his song "The Lighthouse." Ultimately, we would find ourselves living back in our coach.

"Will you look at that Cadillac!" Kenny declared excitedly while staring at the brand new emerald green convertible parked in Rusty's driveway. "It has Rusty's name on the driver's door and his wife's on the other!"

"Kenny?" I asked while carrying our clothes from Rusty's basement, back to the bus. "Do you think we will ever own a car like Rusty's?"

"Maybe," he answered with an air of uncertainty. "I'm not exactly sure what's going to happen right now." His tone had suddenly turned from enthusiastic, to sounding a little depressed.

Somehow, we wanted to believe that everything was going to be all right. Someday, everything would eventually pick up and dates would come in. However, at the moment, things were looking a little bleak for the Hinsons. Finding engagements was like finding the proverbial needle in the haystack.

## LIFE WITH A LEGEND

Kenny and I walked many nights to the Jerry's restaurant, located toward the outskirts of town. There we first experienced the restaurant's strawberry shortcake. We would sometimes stay there for several hours, drinking endless cups of coffee and talking about our future in gospel music. I remember sitting in one of the orange knagohyde booths discussing how desperately we needed things to change. Kenny and I had several long talks while walking back to the bus, which was parked in Mom and Dad's driveway.

In those days, we didn't really understand what it would take to get a break in gospel music. For the most part, we felt somewhat forgotten and abandoned with regard to a music career, and yet by the end of that year, we were able to record our fourth project at Goodman Sound Studios. We called it "He Pilots My Ship."

That same fall, "The Lighthouse" won Song of the Year from The Singing News Fan Awards for the second year running. It was also nominated again in the same category for the Dove Awards. To this day, "The Lighthouse" still remains the only song in gospel music history to win both the Fan Awards and Dove Awards in the same year. Furthermore, in the fall of 1972, it almost did it a second time!

Consequently, these prestigious honors caught the attention of some of gospel music's biggest promoters. Kenny desperately wanted to have his own car. With girlfriends being an ever-present part of his early teenage life, he felt greatly inhibited by not having any personal form of transportation. You can only imagine how excited Kenny was when Aaron Wilburn, who was playing as the Goodman's rhythm guitarist at the time, bought a new car and asked Kenny to drive him around town in it. Aaron had not yet obtained his driver's license and Kenny was more than happy to drive him in return for the privilege of keeping the car and using it as much as he wanted.

By the spring of 1973, the group was beginning to make enough money that we decided to purchase an old two-

# THE BIG MOVE

door beige 1965 Chevrolet Impala. Some of our band members were older than our brother Ronny, and having some form of transportation seemed to be an essential item for them as well.

Latter on, Ked Marcum, a close friend of the family, permitted Kenny to drive his 1969 Plymouth Road Runner indefinitely. By the fall of 1973, Kenny was driving a 1969 burgundy Buick Electra 225. Or what Kenny liked to refer to as his "Deuce and a Quarter." Kenny kept reminding me that one day soon we would be able to get the whole band their very own place to stay. Eventually, we were able to secure a two-bedroom apartment and Kenny moved in with the band, while I moved into a back-porch room at my dad's house.

During this time we managed to make another guest appearance on "The Gospel Singing Jubilee." By the fall of that year, "He Pilots My Ship," won the Song of the Year at the National Quartet Convention. We even got the opportunity to perform the song on stage during the awards ceremony. I'll never forget what Kenny said to me that fall night as we stepped off the stage after singing before thousands of gospel music fans. "Larry, it's happening! This is just the beginning!" I nodded and smiled widely as I thought of the long hard road we had traveled to get here.

It was a whole other world at convention, unlike anything we had ever experienced. We sang with some of these same groups just a couple of years earlier at the Will Rogers auditorium in Fort Worth, Texas, yet they had seen us then as only local yokels and wouldn't give us the time of day. Now we were one of them, well at least nearly. We were just a family group and the quartets were still dominating the field. Nevertheless, Kenny and I felt ten feet tall that night in Nashville, Tennessee. At one point in time, Kenny ran up to me at the record table, where I was taking my turn watching and selling our records. "Larry!" He blurted out as if he were announcing that the building was on fire. "Elvis Presley is back stage right now!"

It was the coolest thing I had ever seen and although we couldn't get anywhere near him for the quartets that surrounded him, it was still so wonderful to be in the presence of such a celebrity! It was not until sometime later that we discovered that the song "The Lighthouse" had been recorded in the movie "Elvis on Tour." We also heard rumors that Rusty Goodman had been able to purchase that gorgeous emerald colored Cadillac as a result of his portion of the publishing royalties for the song.

At the time, it was a bit difficult to watch others financially flourishing around us while we were still basically having bologna as our staple diet. We weren't jealous over the success of others, but we did wonder if we had entered a pond with fish so much bigger than us that we might never see the surface.

Despite the few special appearances we had experienced and the slow influx of engagements for both concerts as well as churches, the career of The Hinsons was still moving at a snail's pace. Many nights Kenny and I lay across from each other on the old iron bunks of that gray colored coach and spoke of the days when someone would truly appreciate our music. Sometimes I cried just a little as a result of what seemed most days like a lost cause. But I knew that Kenny was still clinging to God's promise from five years earlier and that one day He would show everyone in gospel music and all the fans as well, that he had raised us up for a special time. So in the meantime, we just continued to dream.

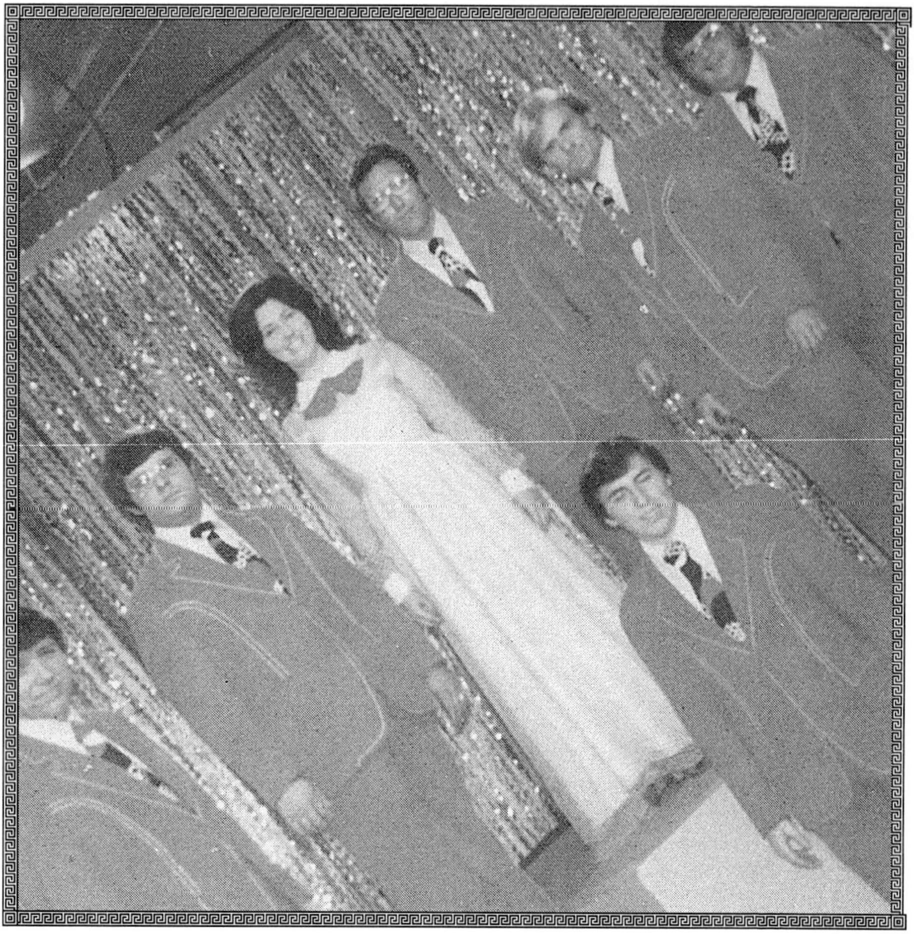

# CHAPTER NINE

## LIGHTS, CAMERAS, ACTION

From 1971 through 1973, Kenny's multi-faceted style of gospel music talent was in full development. For several years, many individuals have attempted to simulate or even imitate Kenny's vocal style. One of the reasons that all of them, without exception, have fallen considerably short of the goal is because they have no working knowledge of what helped to comprise Kenny's sound. To fully understand Kenny's style, you must first realize his many musical influences.

In the early seventies, many Christians still listened to all kinds of pop and country music. For hours upon end, Kenny, Rick Howeth and I, would sit in Kenny's room aboard the gray eagle bus and sing a variety of songs made popular by a vast quantity of secular artists. This may seem somewhat strange to many people in Christendom now, however to this day there are still a number of Nashville's studio musicians who utilize various secular music influences when doing session work for their gospel music clients.

Often times during those engagement-slim days, Rick would grab up the ole box guitar and begin playing a song by the country-rock band The Eagles. Rick would take the lead vocal and Kenny and I would harmonize with him. On many occasions, you could later hear The Eagles' style of word phrasing in something Kenny would sing on record or on stage. Kenny also loved to listen to Roger Miller and during the mid-seventies, he used Roger's influence on such projects as High Voltage. Sometimes, we would sing Beatles' or the Carpenters' songs, which carried a great deal of impact upon Kenny's mindset when we recorded the "Song Vineyard" project in 1980.

So many secular artists including individuals like George Jones gave Kenny some fragment of what would eventually become his own personal style. It wasn't that Kenny desired to sing secular music, it was simply that he believed that he could take the very best of what the world had to offer and give it back to God! In the process, he would also be able to fill a void that existed for those who often only had a steady diet of conventional quartet style music.

Kenny once told our mom that he enjoyed singing with me because I knew what he was thinking and where he was going vocally on stage before he ever got there. The reason I was always able to accomplish that feat was never because I possessed some immense talent. No! The real reason I could predict Kenny's thoughts and vocal inflections is simply because I was there in the beginning and all through the years that his style was being formed.

Kenny always loved to have a good time with music and didn't mind breaking the rules when it came to traditional methods of achieving a desired sound. Often times he operated under the policy that if one could easily sing a particular verse or the lead on the chorus, then they shouldn't be the one to do it. This was because it would inevitably have very little drive or impact on the listener. As a result, you might find yourself surrendering the lead vocals to someone else half way through a chorus, just to add a greater emphasis to a particular line or ending.

Kenny's amazing gift for vocal and musical arrangements easily placed him on the cutting edge of more progressive music for those days. As one major gospel artist would later put it, "Kenny was always before his time." Although most gospel groups may not choose to admit it, they truly owe a great deal to Kenny for pioneering the way in the more progressive southern gospel sounds of today's music. Songs like "Look To Him" and "Here I Grow Again," just to mention a few, helped to blaze a trail for modern gospel artists to follow.

By 1973, Kenny had written and recorded "Ain't That What It's All About," a title that Les Beasley initially made fun of on "The Gospel Singing Jubilee." It was in fact a big hit for Kenny later on, and would eventually become so popular that we had to rerecord it on our "Live" album from Fresno, California.

Although some of Kenny's earlier songs such as "Hey, Lord," would never really spark a genuine interest in his writing abilities, by the time we recorded the "We Promise You Gospel" project in 1973, Kenny was starting to make people sit up and notice his lyrical talents as well.

Somewhere in the middle of that same year, the Happy Goodman Family and "The Gospel Singing Jubilee" came to a parting of the ways. As a result, Les Beasley asked us to join the program as regulars. I'll never forget how Kenny and I jumped up and down at the news of the offer. "I can't believe it!" Kenny kept saying, with all the excitement of a million dollar lottery winner. This was what we had been waiting for and the thrill of having the national exposure that only a program of Jubilee's caliber could bring made us entirely ecstatic!

We eventually realized how hard the work really was, as we actually had to record the show. Produced by Showbiz, the schedule required three consecutive days of filming with three separate shows taped each day. It was early morning work, and often the thick pancake makeup helped to hide everyone's swollen eyes and the sleep lines on their faces.

Kenny would sometimes go into the dressing room at channel 2 where we filmed the show in Nashville and attempt to wake his voice through a process he called vocalizing. For Kenny, that meant starting with his low range notes and eventually working to his highest note. Kenny never wanted any other group's members around when he was vocalizing, as he was so easily embarrassed. Sometimes, however, he would be right in the middle of a high note attempting to, as he put it, "Open his throat," when someone from another group would enter the dressing room without warning. This was always a very awkward moment for Kenny, and he would immediately go deathly quiet and then act as though he had hurt himself and had yelped as a result of the pain. I laughed my head off at him, thinking that everyone knew he was covering up his attempt at waking his voice up. I mean, it wasn't as though everyone else sang perfectly at seven o'clock in the morning anyway. Nonetheless, Kenny was determined to operate in complete denial when necessary and that particularly applied to groups making a guest appearance on the program.

Once he was so startled by someone's unexpected entrance during one of his vocal sessions that his whole body jerked when they walked in. As a result, the coffee in the white Styrofoam cup he was holding spilled on his dress pants. He then tried to wipe the coffee off his leg with the brush of his fingertips and pretend as though all along he had been screaming over the hot liquid pouring on him. Sometimes he was caught doing one of his loud vocal exercises and would immediately go into a short explanation of what he was doing. "Come on in, just warming up the ole vocal chords," he would nervously announce, fully aware that the individual catching him was no doubt doing everything in their power not to laugh.

Strangely enough, no matter how many vocal frequencies Kenny seemed to be lacking in the dressing room, by the time he stepped in front of the cameras his voice operated as if it had simply been waiting for the cue and he almost always hit the mark dead on. More than once, Kenny suffered from a bad case of strep throat and yet, he was still able to sing incredibly well even while in pain! I'm not exactly sure why Kenny had so many bouts with the viral infection or with bronchitis for that matter. The only thing that I could ever really associate with the reason for his frequent illnesses was the fact that he was so very sick as a child and had to have his tonsils removed early in life.

We filmed the Jubilee for the next several years, and as a result, our popularity soared higher and higher in the realms of southern gospel music. Jana Hartley, whom I had initially met in Ontario, California two years earlier, and whom I had only seen once more during our 1972 California tour, now watched us faithfully every Sunday morning. It made me feel so warm inside to think that she, along with many other people across the nation, were tuning in to hear us sing every weekend.

Jana and I were writing steadily by this time and Kenny always made it a point to bring me her letters whenever possible so he could tease me about my liking her so much. "You've got a letter from the water girl," he would remark sarcastically. Kenny referred to her as "The water girl" because of our initial meeting over the water glass in the prayer box. I kept her picture in clear view of my bed on the bus at all times and Kenny was fully aware that I was more serious about my feelings for her than any other girl I'd ever known.

Kenny had a main girlfriend as well at the time and when we were in her hometown in Mississippi I did my fair share of teasing him right back. It was certainly true that the enormous amount of popularity associated with being gospel music television stars had its advantages. Especially when it came to having girl friends!

Kenny found himself spending a great deal of the small amounts of money available to him on everything from buying roses to special gifts for his many female acquaintances. Making the right impression upon the opposite sex seemed to be a priority for Kenny at that time.

By the spring of 1974, things were changing dramatically for other relationships in our group. Soon, Kenny would find himself right in the middle of an uncomfortable situation with our bass player Rick Howeth.

For a couple of years, Rick and our sister Yvonne had privately shared feelings for one another. Ronny and Kenny decided that they should not go public with their relationship as it might result in some unseemly rumors within the gospel music industry. Rick and Yvonne initially agreed to stay quiet about their feelings and to postpone any marriage plans for an indefinite period. But no sooner had Ronny and Kenny given their consent for wedding plans to commence, than Yvonne suddenly realized that she was not really in love and broke off the relationship altogether. This was a hard pill for Rick to swallow. As a result, he was deeply wounded at both Ronny and Kenny, feeling that they had ruined his marriage plans by forcing them to wait as a couple.

It wasn't too long before Yvonne's love interests turned toward another guy named David Johnson that she eventually married. I suppose that the pressure was far too much for Rick to bear. He was still in love with Yvonne and wasn't about to stick around while she became the wife of someone else. Unfortunately, Kenny didn't quite understand such feelings at the time and couldn't understand why Rick would abandon the group during such a crucial time in our career.

I was standing in the stairwell of the bus when Kenny confronted Rick as he attempted to get his bags off our coach to take a bus back home to California. I suppose because Kenny saw Rick as somewhat of a brother to him he felt personally betrayed at Rick's abrupt departure. Yet at the time, Rick was greatly embittered over Kenny's role in his losing Yvonne and when Kenny pressed the issue that day on the bus, a fistfight nearly ensued between them.

We had long since hired another piano player by the name of Robert. Robert had obviously made a specific point of stirring up bad feelings between Kenny and Rick. Robert always complained about everything we group leaders did and was usually involved with a lot of behind the scene discord where the band was concerned.

## LIFE WITH A LEGEND

Shortly after Rick's initial decision to leave the group, Robert helped organize a last minute stage walk off that resembled a codetta more than just a normal strike. It would not have been so bad, except that Robert waited to enact his power play right as we were at our most vulnerable moment. Just as the master of ceremonies introduced the Hinsons to the stage in concert one night in Knoxville, Tennessee, almost the entire band refused to go on unless an agreement was instantly reached with regard to salaries.

Kenny showed his true metal that evening, faced with the choice of either paying a specific amount to each band member, or losing his on stage band in a flash. He wasted no time in grabbing up his guitar and then turning to Ronny and I, he sternly announced, "Let's sing family!" With that, Kenny, Ronny, Yvonne, our only remaining musician Arnie and I walked on stage, to a stunned but very receptive audience. Kenny was appalled that the band members saw money as more important than the ministry.

On more than one occasion, Kenny was forced to put that concept to the test in his own personal life, as a variety of country music offers came his way. By the summer of 1974, Yvonne was married and expecting a child. Her doctor had by and large, forced her off the road, due to complications with the pregnancy. Suddenly, we were faced with the major dilemma of finding a replacement for Yvonne.

Poor Kenny was weighted down with the immense pressure of rehearsing every single applicant for the position. People came from just about everywhere in the United States to try out. Since Kenny was the music and vocal master of the group, he felt responsible for each and every audition.

Finally, it was decided that a young seventeen-year-old girl from California named Chris Hawkins would fill the available slot. Kenny worked tirelessly to reshape and intensify the inexperienced artist's qualities. Sometimes his methods reminded me of that the old black and white movie "Phantom of the Opera" as on more than one occasion Kenny seemed more concerned with Chris' perfection than her feelings. The way Kenny saw it, he could either sympathize with someone's feelings, or help to make them the very best they could be. For this reason, every person that has ever been truly successful in the music field due to his input remains deeply grateful for Kenny's relentless push during their personal years under his training.

Kenny scolded more than one of our musicians on stage for not taking the proper amount of time to tune his instrument before walking out in front of and audience to perform. Kenny was also very concerned about phrasing and diction when it came to singing a song. This was particularly true when we recorded a project in the one of the many studios in the Nashville area.

This was also a time in my life when I worked extremely hard to gain Kenny's confidence and approval as an artist. Kenny was still his private jovial self off stage and yet he began to feel the ever increasing pressure to set some kind of standard for excellence in gospel music on stage and in the studio. As a result, he often rode each of us fairly hard about syncopating our lines or pronouncing our words precisely, sometimes to the point of exaggerating the line altogether.

He also made a strong effort to secure his place as the lead vocalist of the group by becoming extremely guarded in preserving the strongest country gospel emphasis exclusively for him self. Kenny was beginning to feel trapped in what he felt, at the time, was the necessary commercialism of our music. For this reason, he started performing and recording with primarily one focus at all times: "Someone's listening, be your very best!"

During the early 1970s Kenny first began taking a strong interest in producing our recording projects as well as performing on them. Kenny later had a couple of his own small record labels: "Fire Heart" and "Light Heart Records."

After the band strike of 1974, Kenny left the band's apartment and moved into the room at my parents' house that had initially been occupied by Yvonne. Although Kenny was still his sweet and humorous self to all newer band members, he never again would allow the same feelings of closeness that had been present in the first full band of the early seventies. Kenny always continued to be extremely in touch with the feelings of the group's musicians. Yet, he would no longer permit himself to get too comfortable with a band member or forget that those he had felt were much like family had betrayed him. For this reason, he always remained in the roll of the boss to some degree from then on.

After Chris Hawkins joined the group and we went through an almost complete band transition the Hinsons decided to take part in the maiden voyage of the singings at sea. Along with many of the groups from the Jubilee program, the Hinsons set sail for the Bahamas.

It was an exciting voyage to say the least. Kenny stood by me on the open deck, next to the massive swimming pool as we stared out across the vast ocean that first night aboard the S. S. Bahamas Star. The full moon spilled its glowing light across the white caped waves and the fleecy clouds displayed a bluish shine with a golden lining around each one. "This is beautiful Larry!" Kenny said excitedly, as the warm ocean breeze ruffled his heavily sprayed hair.

"You're not kiddin'," I replied in an equally excited tone, placing my fingers in either side of my back pockets. I knew that Kenny had just been through a tremendous ordeal with the band and that this trip would provide a much-needed rest for him, even if we had to sing for our boat ride. I was in charge of booking the voyage for the group and for the guests who had joined the cruise as friends of The Hinsons, so I was able to make sure that Kenny and I shared a cabin together. Even though we each had a bunk back in our cabin, Kenny and I couldn't seem to go to bed. We just kept walking the decks and exploring the ship! Even though we had taken some pills in order to prevent nausea, we found it impossible to get sleepy.

The next morning we docked in Nassau. Jerry Trammel of The Florida Boys told us of some motorbikes that were available for rent on shore. Kenny hurried on ahead with Jerry to check out the scooters, as Arnie and I followed them down the gangplank at a distance. As I was disembarking from the ship, I couldn't help but notice that the village market place lay straight ahead. I quickly scanned the pottery and baskets at the foot of the gangplank. "This place," I said to myself, "is certainly tropical in every way!"

Just then, a Bahamian at the end of the gangplank, asked me if I wanted some coke. To which I promptly and kindly replied, "No thank you, I'm not thirsty."

"No!" the man bellowed, as though I had offended him in some way. He waved me on with his left hand and quickly turned his attention toward another man behind Arnie and me. Arnie nearly fell off the gangplank laughing at me and once we were far enough away from the drug dealer to speak freely, Arnie informed me that the man was referring to cocaine. My eyes, no doubt, got as big around as one of the basket lids in the market place.

"Not me!" I responded, shocked, as if Arnie was attempting to sell the white powder to me as well.

We all rented motorbikes and began touring the island's entire twenty-one mile length. Driving on the left side of the road proved to be more than a little challenge for me. I didn't realize that the Bahamas were under British rule until I peeled out from the rental shop. It didn't take long for me to get confused in the traffic as to which side of the road I was supposed to be on and I ran into the back of a parked Volkswagen Beetle. I thought Kenny and Jerry would never stop laughing. Fortunately, Arnie wasn't with us at the moment, or I would have never heard the last of it.

During that particular trip we also docked on the island of Freeport. The dock was a few miles from town and the cabbies were to expensive to do much traveling back and forth between the ship and the village. The most exciting aspect of the cruise came when we had the opportunity to sing for the Governor of the Bahamas, in the Governor's Hall. With little money and the lack of sleep overtaking us, Kenny and I decided to grab a quick bite in the dinning room and then hit the sack for a couple of hours. The dining hall was jammed packed with people when we arrived and it took over an hour to finally get seated. Once inside, our eyes became overwhelmed with the massive quantities and selections of food displayed on the lengthy buffet. That was where I had my first experience with Baked Alaska. Kenny and I thought we had died and gone to heaven!

Singing in the lounge area during the group's concert appearance was quite an enjoyable experience as well. Because the passengers on the cruise were mostly Christians, the bar served only soft drinks during the entire cruise. Kenny and I ordered Shirley Temples when it wasn't our time to sing and we sat around chatting with fans and artists alike.

As we stepped off the ship in Miami, Florida at the end of the cruise, Kenny remarked, "We've got to do this again!"

"Yeah," I replied in voice filled with great anticipation. "Real soon!" I added as we walked further from the dock towards the parking lot where our coach was waiting. Little did we know then that this would be our only voyage together.

By 1975, Kenny was adding a steady stream of his own songs to our recordings. "Once Again" was included on the second project with Chris Hawkins entitled "Harvest of Hits." However "Home Sick to Go," written by Ronny, was Kenny's real song of notoriety that year. By this time, Kenny was already pretty serious about just one girl, Debbie Mysinger. His frequent trips to Chattanooga, Tennessee where she lived kept him busy and away from the rest of us when we weren't on the road as a group. Kenny was acting more and more distant towards everyone in the family and yet I seemed to feel the widening space more than the rest.

Yvonne reassured me that this sort of thing happened a lot where guys were concerned when serious relationships developed with women. For me though, knowing this was little consolation. I was losing my big brother to someone else and it was difficult to deal with. "You've changed," I remember telling Kenny, late one night on the bus as we were returning home from a long week of engagements.

"In what way?" Kenny replied with an obvious air of confusion in his voice.

"I don't know," I replied shrugging my shoulders and lifting my eyebrows slightly. "I guess, you're never around anymore and you don't seem to have time for me like you used to."

"Well," Kenny responded with frustration. "You'll know what it feels like to really be in love some day and when that happens, nothing or no one will be as important to you as your true love is!" His words made perfect sense to me and yet I couldn't help feeling like our relationship would never be the same. Soon, that feeling would prove to be right!

# CHAPTER TEN

## A TIME OF DISCOVERY

By the winter of 1974, I had fallen madly in love with the short dark headed girl Kenny jokingly called "The Water Girl." Jana had moved to Oklahoma City, Oklahoma to be closer to me in Kentucky. She was attending Southwestern Bible College and she drove to see me whenever I was in the area. When Christmas rolled around that year, I sent her a plane ticket and asked her to join me for the holidays. I felt that this would be a good opportunity for her to get more acquainted with my family. Kenny and I had picked her up at the airport.

She naturally thought we were a big success in gospel music. When we got to our house at 1077 Grapevine Road she got out of the car and starting walking straight for Rusty's house. Kenny immediately started cracking up. "You need to stop her Larry!" Kenny chided with a chuckle in his voice. "You didn't tell her that we live in the old shack?" What an embarrassment!

It was during this particular visit that I asked Jana to be exclusive with me and gave her a promise ring. I felt that we had both truly enjoyed her Christmas visit and that she was indeed the right one for me. It was incredibly difficult to take her back to the airport when it came time for her to go back to Oklahoma.

# A TIME OF DISCOVERY

Kenny drove Jana and I back to the airport that winter in his burgundy deuce and a quarter. Kenny kept wiping the fog off his windows due to all the kissing going on in the back seat. "You guys are gonna have to let up for a little while!" He announced with a joking expression in his eyes now peering back at us through the rear view mirror. "My defroster is broken and I can't see a thing." For the very first time I truly realized, Kenny had been right when he told me that I would act different too, once I fell in love. I could not imagine how I ever lived without her and immediately started thinking about marriage.

Jana had been thinking along these lines since the early days of our relationship. It had taken me quite a bit longer than her and a trip to visit her in her California home early that summer in order to change my way of thinking. That trip had made my brother Ronny extremely angry though because he didn't want me to chase after some girl who might not be willing to marry me and still allow me to stay in the group. He and most of the rest of my family had done in everything in their power to discourage my relationship with Jana, sighting their ever-present intuition that Jana was really after Kenny and not me.

Getting laryngitis during the cold atmosphere on the return plane flight didn't seem to help my situation any. I was forced under contractual agreements to continue singing despite doctor's orders to rest for two weeks. Eventually I lost my voice altogether and had to sit on an inhalation machine full of prescription drugs, something I had to do before each concert in order to sing at all.

Kenny had to try out a number of other amateur artists in an attempt to find someone that could take my place. Poor Ronny Moore, our steel guitarist, was forced to sing most of the second half of each program in my stead. It was extremely strenuous on him to say the least and unbelievably frustrating for Kenny as well.

By the time we drove back to the airport after Christmas, I still wasn't completely healed or back in full swing. For this reason, I felt my economical future needed some improvement before I could even think of settling down with Jana. "Think you'll marry her?" Kenny asked all at once over the noisy crowd passing by in the nearby corridor as Jana entered the accordion hallway to board the big bird.

"I'm thinking about it!" I replied quickly, in a nervous tone.

"The reason I asked you, was because I've noticed that lately you've changed." Suddenly, I glanced in his direction and from the corner of my eye I caught the slightest smirk starting to form on his lips.

"Aah, shut up!" I responded with a chuckle.

By the next year, way before Christmas that year Kenny had announced to the family his intentions of marrying Debbie. We were informed that they were taking it slow and that they were considering the summer of 1976 as a wedding date. During Christmas in 1975, I had given Jana an engagement ring.

By January of 1976, the group had solidified plans to tour California again in the spring of the year. As soon as I received the news, I put in a call to Jana's dorm at the college and shared my ideas with her for a spring wedding. She had only been back at school for a short time and despite the advice from her mother not to return to school but to prepare to get married soon she had chosen to return to Oklahoma instead.

I explained to Jana over the phone that April would be an ideal month to get married. Not only would most of my family be present for our wedding, but our band would be there to play live music for the ceremony as well. I didn't tell her at the time that I had every intention of singing a song to her that I had written specifically for the occasion. I felt as if a live band would add the necessary touch making it even more special. Jana eventually agreed to the spring wedding and flew home for all the essential preparations.

Within just a few short days of announcing my plans to marry Jana in April of that year, Kenny and Debbie announced their plans to exchange their wedding vows in March instead of in the summer. This would place their wedding almost exactly one month before my wedding date. Suddenly, I felt as if I was ten years old again instead of nineteen and once again I was struggling for sibling placement with my older brother. I suppose for some reason, Kenny felt that it would not be appropriate to allow his little brother to marry before he did. As a result, his wedding plans were announced in *The Singing News Magazine* before mine.

Now I felt, I was being forced to follow his example instead of the other way around. On March 7, 1976, Kenny and Debbie were married in Soddy Daisy, Tennessee. On April 6, 1976, Jana and I were married in Ontario, California. I could already feel a small gulf beginning to form between Kenny and me and therefore requested that he stand up for me at my wedding as my best man.

Mom no doubt felt as if she had been hit with a double whammy. No sooner had she gotten over the tears of losing one son to marriage, than she lost a second son within a month. From that moment on, Kenny grew even more distant towards me as he began to settle into his new world of married life.

In the summer of that same year, we recorded an album called "High Voltage" that included my very first attempt at song writing. "Lord Remember Me" was less than memorable, however, I was proud to finally join my brothers in the ranks as a writer. I had strong hopes of utilizing my talents to help subsidize my income. Kenny on the other hand, was already cranking out such hits as "Campmeeting Days." I was proud of Kenny and yet a little envious also.

In a sense, marriage made both Kenny and I serious contenders for getting a song on our newest projects. Ronny pretty much dominated the few available slots on any given album we were planning to record because of his already proven talent. This in turn, left very little space for anyone else to include a song of his or her own. Ronny was indeed the most accomplished lyricist of the group and the record company naturally felt he should have first shot at the number of songs he placed on a project. Kenny felt that he was the second most accomplished writer and therefore he should have seniority over me. I knew that I couldn't continue to write low caliber songs like my first one if I ever intended to gain their respect as a writer and have a strong voice in song placement on any of our future projects.

Jana couldn't understand why brothers couldn't simply share equally, a view that my mother had always possessed as well. It was difficult for me to help Jana understand that in gospel music and in our family it didn't work that way. Because there were so many watching our accomplishments and because the gospel music industry judged each of us based upon our past achievements or failures, I would have to wait and prove myself before getting the proper respect I desired.

Regardless of the jockeying for position that existed during those early days of ministry, Kenny never allowed the competition to damper his anointing one single bit and neither did I. Affecting a life or winning a soul for Christ was far too important to permit any personal conflicts to hinder our efforts on stage. I don't mean to leave the impression that Kenny and I fought in any way, quite the contrary. In fact, Kenny was so completely non-confrontational that the most annoying thing to me was that I couldn't get him to talk things out at all. In addition, his marital relationship strongly encouraged increasing secrecy about everything he said or did. Everything was on a need to know basis only.

In addition, if I bought a new car, Kenny soon showed up with either a newer car or at least a bigger and more expensive car than mine. It is somewhat strange the way that individuals view relationships when they're still young. Priorities seem so very different when you haven't yet found the recognition that every person so strongly craves. What seemed so important to each of us back then, became, over time, the least of our concerns.

Kenny was becoming so popular by this point that many of the major artists gathered at the curtain wings of the concerts in order to listen to his far-reaching vocal capabilities. Where once he had watched Howard and Vestal Goodman from backstage, now he was the individual being watched. More than once I heard someone hanging around backstage comment, "Man, that boy can sing!" Yet Kenny seemed to manage it all with an air of modesty. On more than one occasion, both his vocal talents and his powerful anointing literally brought the house down. Yet when it came time for the audience to applaud his efforts, he would just point his index finger heavenward as if to indicate that the Lord was the one worthy of their applause.

By the fall of 1976, Kenny's reputation had become so wide spread that the gospel music industry could no longer deny his presence. As a matter of fact, he was pioneering a whole category of southern gospel music. That year, Kenny received the award for Favorite Lead Vocalist from The Singing News Fan Awards, the only time it was ever held in Dallas, Texas. From that moment on, Kenny's fame increased even more rapidly. In 1977, I was nominated for Favorite Baritone by The Singing News.

We were on our way to sing at an engagement near Miami, Oklahoma, when our bus caught on fire. Some wiring in Ronny's closet had somehow sparked a flame amidst his clothes and soon the entire room was in flames. Jana and I had purchased several articles of clothing to wear during the prestigious week of the National Quarter Convention. Everything we had went up in flames as we watched helplessly from outside the coach. Of course, we were far from being alone in our little dilemma. Most everything on the bus went up in smoke, all except the sound equipment in the luggage bins below the floor level of the bus.

Our bus was not equipped with a restroom at the time. Many of the gospel groups back in those days still stopped to use public restrooms instead of having one on their bus. Kenny decided to keep around a sealed plastic milk jug just in case he was ever in an emergency situation where there were no bathrooms available. But as the old adage goes, "So much for good intentions." He kept finding himself in emergency situations so often that when the bus caught on fire, the fireman discovered his plastic milk jug filled nearly to the top.

The funny thing was the fireman thought it was gasoline and nearly panicked getting one of the bus' side windows open. He ordered all of us to stand back while he tossed the so-called gasoline to the surface of the blacktop parking lot. Kenny let out a loud yelp as it impacted and burst open. I immediately chimed in with laughter, knowing full well that the content was by no means gasoline. Simultaneous laughter broke out throughout the entire group as everyone finally realized what the fireman had actually disposed of.

Within just a few short days we were standing in Birmingham, Alabama at the National Quartet Convention where I received the award for Favorite Baritone from the Fan Awards. "Just think," Kenny said humorously, while taking the award from my hand backstage so that he could examine it more closely. "You've been given an award in category you don't even sing in." His tenor now exhibited a tiny measure of sarcasm, as he continued to look at the large silver dish from every conceivable angle. "Can you imagine how many awards you'll win for first tenor, once somebody figures out that that's what you actually sing most of the time?" Kenny just smirked and congratulated me on a more serious note and then threw his long arm around my shoulder and squeezed me tightly to him. "I'm proud of you, Larry!" Kenny added sincerely.

As the remaining years of the seventies went by, Kenny and I grew closer again. He continued to sweep many of the awards ceremonies with his incomparable vocal talents. We recorded several more albums, which featured many number one hits due to his incredible voice. And I gave in to the idea that he was meant to be the shining star of our group. I also came to realize that I was meant to help him shine. I

# A TIME OF DISCOVERY

truly came to recognize that Kenny was a sort of military commander to me and I actually began to appreciate the privilege of standing beside him on stage each night!

# CHAPTER ELEVEN

# THE NATION'S NUMBER ONE GROUP

On August 2, 1978, Jana and I had our first child we named Larry Hinson, Jr. "Little Larry," as he was affectionately called, had difficulty breathing at birth because he was delivered two weeks prematurely. He was born at the Seventh Day Adventist Hospital in Madison, Tennessee. Ronny stayed with me at the hospital that August while the rest of the group initially went to our engagement, thinking we would soon fly out to meet them in Oklahoma.

Harold drove the group almost all the way to their destination when the state troopers in Oklahoma flagged them down. It was then that everyone aboard our private coach received the news that there had been some complications with Little Larry's breathing and that neither Ronny nor I would be leaving town. Too spent from the long journey he had driven, Harold handed over the driver's seat to Kenny who stayed faithfully behind the wheel of the bus all the way back to Nashville. Although exhausted from the all night trek back home, Kenny managed to drag himself down to the hospital where he was a tremendous support to Jana and me.

I will never forget his encouragement during that time when things looked so hopeless for Little Larry's survival. Even while our pastor was telling us to prepare for the funeral, Kenny was persuading me to trust in God for a miracle. Partially because of Kenny's faith and strength, I was able to mount the bus that same week and fulfill our engagements with every confidence that God would heal my son. Even though the doctors told us that his chances of living were slim and that he would remain under treatment for at least three months, I continued to believe.

I remember coming down the bus aisle that week and rounding the corner that led from the private bedrooms, only to find Kenny sitting on the couch in the bus lobby. He was playing his box guitar and singing an old church song from a by gone era, "Hold to God's Unchanging Hand." Kenny knew how to not only encourage himself in the Lord, but those around him as well. I couldn't help but join him in with him on the chorus. We sang several other songs of faith and healing, and Kenny reminded me that we served a healing God!

When I returned home just four days after my son's birth, my wife informed me that Little Larry had suddenly gotten well and that we were being permitted to pick him up from the hospital that very afternoon. I called Kenny and informed him of the news and we rejoiced together!

After that particular incident, Kenny and I grew closer on a spiritual level as well as a personal level. I had continued to preach over the years since my initial calling in 1967. Kenny was still yearning to fulfill that side of his personal ministry as well. His hunger to draw closer to the Lord seemed to be a feeling that preoccupied his mind quite frequently at the time. We started having prayer meetings at my place and Kenny renewed his seeking to be filled with the Holy Ghost. He wanted to be filled and start preaching.

I'll never forget how he lay behind my chocolate colored velvet couch and tearfully spoke in a heavenly language. He even did a little prophesying as well! By 1979, Kenny's first child Amanda was born. It was a proud day for Kenny, especially because he truly loved children in general and now he would be able to shower his own offspring with all his unbridled affection. I have never seen anyone that loved his or her children in the same way Kenny did.

As a matter of fact, Kenny loved his children almost to a fault. At times, he would let them slide in areas where they really needed discipline. He once told me this was because he was always gone and didn't want to spend his few moments with his kids spanking and scolding them.

I was of a completely different mind-set when it came to discipline. I felt that the only way I would not create a conflict in our home by undermining the rules my wife set, was by attempting to enforce what she and I had agreed upon. I would sometimes shake my head at Kenny in disbelief when at a restaurant he would permit his children to order full size meals from the menu instead of ordering off the children's menu like my kids. Both his children would ultimately wind up taking a few small bites of their dinner and then commence to want desert.

The same year Amanda was born, another miraculous thing happened. At the National Quartet Convention that fall, it became official that God had kept a long-standing promise to The Hinsons. We were voted The Nation's Number One Group!

The celebration had hardly started dying down when countless offers for engagements began flowing into our office. We were even able to increase the amount of money we received for a single performance! "He did it!" Kenny whispered in my ear, with an excitement to his voice that night at the Fan Awards. "God kept his promise, Larry!" His eyes filled with tears as he threw his arm around my neck and pulled me close to his chest like he had so many times in the early years. For a moment, I felt small again and thought about the first conversation we exchanged on the old yellow school bus over a decade before.

Everyone in gospel music had his or her eyes on us from that time on. Even the country music promoters and record label producers started making offers because of the notoriety it afforded us.

By 1980, Chris Hawkins had left the group to get married and our sister Yvonne stepped back into her old position. Also that year, a major record label and country music promoter placed a multi-facetted offer before us to sing "middle of the road" music. It proved to be quite tempting, to say the least.

My wife Jana, however, was dead set against accepting the offer because she felt that it was nothing more than a ploy to get us completely away from singing gospel music. Despite her unwillingness to play along, I decided to take my chances with the rest of my siblings and prepare myself for the new direction I was able to explore. While sitting in the office of the well-known country artist that was also the president of the record label, we were privileged to meet one of country music's biggest promoters at the time.

For a while everything seemed to go as planned until an unexpected visitor showed up at the meeting. No one in the office knew he was coming, however, later I discovered that my own wife had sent him to disrupt the meeting. Between the producer and us, we decided that we would use a song that I had written for our very first single in this new music market. The promoter offered us thousands of dollars each week for concert performances and the record producer offered us even more for the recordings. There were also the royalties from the airplay on radio stations and from BMI to consider.

The only problem was, the uninvited guest my wife had sent down to interrupt the meeting was doing quite a good job. He kept talking while I was trying to listen to the president of the record company. The more I strained to hear the producer, the louder the visitor talked.

The strange thing was, no one else could hear him but me. I suppose the Holy Spirit had come to that meeting to stop the whole procedure. It was working! All at once, the Spirit of God asked me a question I could neither ignore nor answer. "How do you plan to sing country music and preach

My gospel?" It seemed to make little difference to him that we called it MOR (Middle of the Road) music.

Suddenly I stood to my feet and stepped out of the office there on music row and walked outside to the veranda. I stared at the ground for what seemed like only a short period of time when one of the producer's associates came outside to inquire about my well being. "Are you all right, Larry?" the deep base voice boomed from behind me. I spun around quickly to notice Don Brake with a rather concerned expression on his face.

"No, Don," I said softly, not caring that my voice had cracked as I responded.

"What's wrong?" Don persisted, attempting not to appear nervous about my potential for blowing a very lucrative record and promotional package. "Whatever it is, I'm sure we can work it out." His words were hardly able to mask the trembling in his voice. Don knew that something was terribly wrong and he obviously had been involved with enough music negotiations to realize that this time he was going to have to count on sheer hype to get me back inside. "Hey buddy, if we've said something about your song that offended you, or if you don't feel like you have the opportunity to voice your opinion strongly enough, I'm certain it's negotiable," he continued almost frantically.

"Don," I replied in a volume level barely above a whisper, "I'll go back inside with you and continue the negotiations if you can answer me one question."

"Hey friend, I'll do my very best," Don replied uneasily.

"Don, you're a preacher's son right?"

"Right," Don answered slowly, while no doubt waiting for the other shoe to drop so to speak.

"Tell me Don, how can I preach and sing country music too?" Don's face dropped like it had suddenly been attached to a ninety-pound weight.

"You do have a problem don't you?" Don was now rubbing his chin with the inside of his right index finger and the tip of his right thumb. His face was that of someone in total confusion. Now it was he who was staring at the grass of the veranda.

"Tell them thanks, but no thanks. I'm going home," I said.

After about an hour, Kenny arrived at my place, fit to be tied. I really didn't blame him. After all, he saw the offer as an opportunity to make the kind of money that gospel music could never possibly afford us. Yet, I knew that I couldn't go through with the deal and preach as well.

From that moment forward I decided in my heart to go back to my first love of ministry. Not because I couldn't possibly match the song writing talents of Ronny or the singing abilities of Kenny, no, the real reason I needed to pursue the preaching of the gospel was because it was simply my strongest calling. For this reason I informed Kenny and Ronny that I would be leaving the family sometime within the next couple of years.

By February of 1981, Jana and I had added a new addition to our family. We were graciously blessed with our only daughter. We decided to name her Lyndi. It was around this same time that Kenny wanted me to give him a more specific date for my departure from the group. Jana and I agreed to leave the family on August 2, 1981.

With this newly acquired information, Kenny set out to discover a male-vocalist who could fill my slot. After several failed attempts at finding someone capable of stepping into the vacancy Kenny finally settled on our older brother Calvin's son Eric.

Kenny grew increasingly angry towards me as the date of my departure got closer. By the time we made our last bus ride home together that year, Kenny looked at me from his propped position atop his upper bunk bed and asked me the question, "How can you do this to me?" His voice displayed both anger and hurt.

"I'm not trying to do anything to you Kenny," I replied mildly. "I'm just trying to obey God!" Kenny's expression demonstrated sheer frustration and disgust.

Within just a few short days, Jana and I were making plans to move to Oklahoma where we felt that the Lord was leading us to go. Kenny showed up to watch us loading the moving van. But to demonstrate his protest of the move, he refused to help me pack in any way. Later that same day, Jana reminded me that Kenny still loved me but that right then he was hurt and angry. I could only pray that healing would come soon!

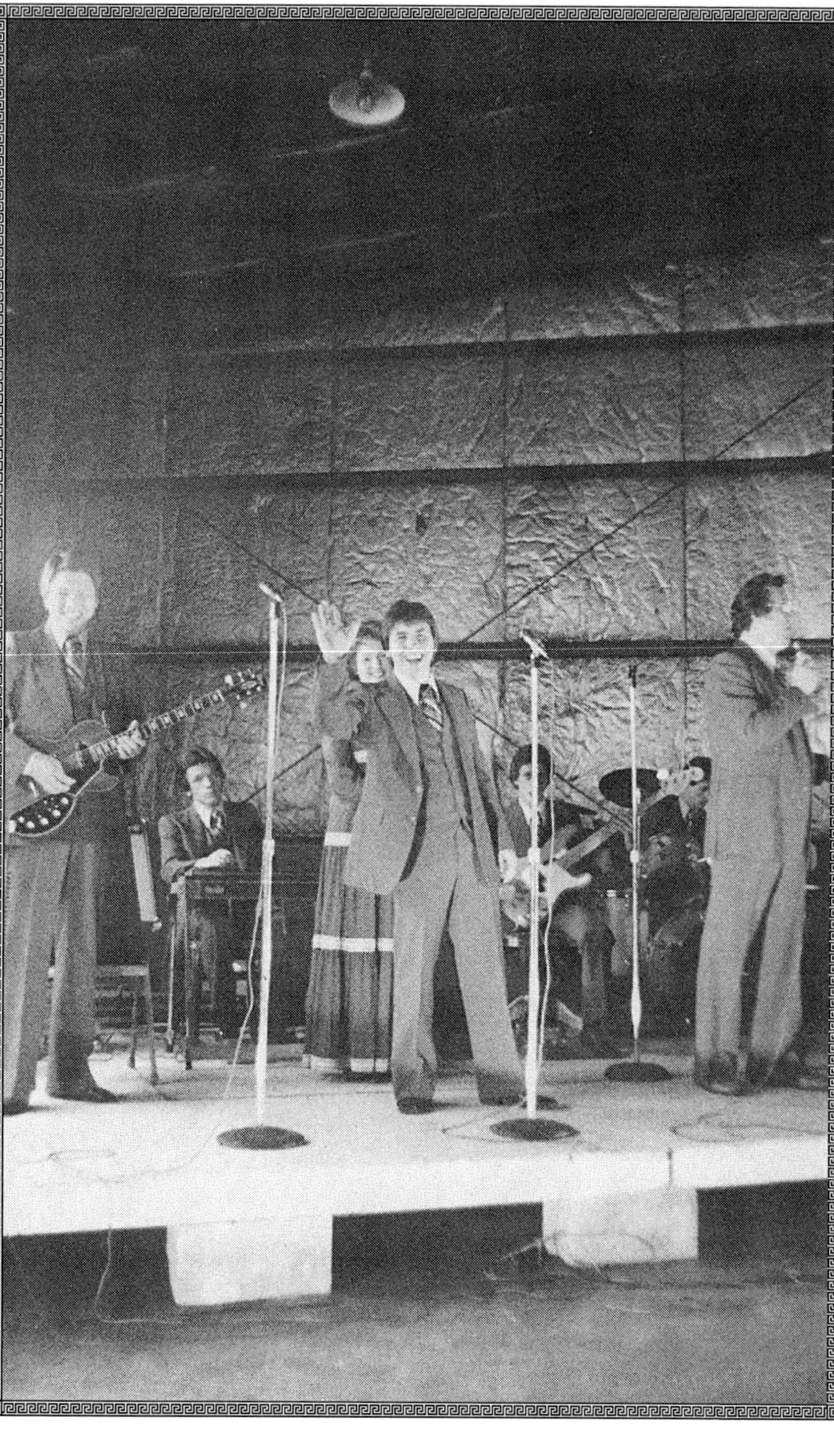

# CHAPTER TWELVE

## JOSEPH AND HIS BROTHERS

By September of 1981, Jana and I were living in Eufaula, Oklahoma. All four of us in our family were forced to live in a single bedroom at the home of a college friend of Jana's. At the time Jana and I were flat broke, and most of the engagements we had scheduled with pastors earlier that year had canceled without notice at the last minute. Pastors who had once spoken with me at a concert where we initially scheduled our revival meeting with them now strangely enough couldn't even remember my name. It was becoming quite apparent to me that these particular pastors only wanted me while I remained in the limelight of southern gospel music.

It didn't take very long to discover that these same pastors who loved to hear me sing may have also been scared to death of what doctrine I might preach behind their pulpits. I also found out quickly enough that those same kind of pastors had no problem paying a major gospel singing group a flat rate for coming to their church to sing, however, they fully expected the evangelist to come and preach for only a free-will offering. What hypocrisy, I thought. Those pastors were only after the notoriety a popular singing group could bring to them and not what the spoken word could do for their congregations.

I found myself unable to even buy a free-will offering engagement. I was finally offered an opportunity to follow a friend around to his Pentecostal Church of God youth rallies and preach. After several other offerings were taken each time, my friend would finally receive one for me. Most of the time, they amounted to about twenty-five to fifty dollars. I was so grateful to the Lord to be receiving anything by this point that I couldn't bring myself to complain, even though I knew that I couldn't pay my bills for the most part.

I also came to understand just how unimportant I really had been to the success of The Hinsons in the first place. Evangelism was a field of ministry I would have to build altogether from scratch.

It was a humbling time for me and for my immediate family. Jana and I finally managed to afford a little rental house in the country. Sometimes we had no money to keep the air on in the summer or the heat on in the winter. Groceries were also a major problem from time to time during the first year of evangelism.

One of my cousins came to visit me at from Little Rock, Arkansas only to discover that we had no propane in our propane tank outside to keep the house heated. We were all wrapped up in blankets attempting to stay warm. He also discovered that we had no diapers for our youngest child and no milk or baby food for either of our children. As a matter of fact, the only thing to eat in the entire house that winter's day was one moldy yellow onion and two large cans of Swanson's chicken broth. We did a whole lot of weeping and crying out to God for help during my cousin's visit and the next morning bright and early, he headed back to the safety and sanity of Little Rock, but not before eating one of the cans of chicken broth. Many times I wanted to just quit the ministry and get a regular job.

God did finally send someone by our house to bless us with money for propane, food and diapers. After a few months, engagements started to pick up a little at least to the place where we didn't need to rely on someone to turn our heat on or buy us some groceries. By the time Kenny finally came to hear me preach, he found Jana and I ministering at a small country church in West Memphis, Arkansas. The building was old and run down and the crowd that night was incredibly small.

All Kenny could do during my sermon was to sit in on his back row seat and shake his head in disbelief. I felt quite embarrassed to say the least, when he asked what I was doing in a place where no one cared enough to even come out to hear me preach. I tried to explain to Kenny that some people just like singing and don't want to hear a preacher. Kenny wasn't buying it at all. All through the remaining minutes of their stay at the meeting, Kenny just kept silently shaking his head towards the ground in disbelief.

I was so very humiliated when they asked us after service if we wanted to go get a bite to eat somewhere. We had two small children and barely any money to eat on for the entire revival. There was no way we were financially capable of splurging on an additional late night dinner. We were just in hopes that the pastor might ask us over to his house for a bologna sandwich. Kenny had brought his wife and daughter with him that night and he was also carrying the latest addition to his family, Kenneth Weston Hinson.

Although the tension over the issue of my leaving the group had not yet been resolved, Kenny had evidently wanted us to see our new nephew. Kenny decided to spend the night at the same motel where we were staying for the revival and the next morning he and I had breakfast alone together. I'll never forget how much like a failure I felt when he made his closing remarks before leaving for Nashville. "Larry," he said sincerely, "if you ever need anything, let me know." His voice carried an almost inquisitive sound, as if he fully expected me to start naming my needs immediately. "I mean, don't stay out here and starve!" he cautioned further.

"We're doing just fine Kenny, really!" I spoke in as convincing a tone as possible, but I really wasn't sure if he truly believed me. He must have chalked my response up to foolish pride and simply chose to raise his eyebrows slowly, simultaneously pursing his lips. Shortly after breakfast Kenny gathered his family together and headed back to Nashville.

Several months passed before I had the opportunity to see Kenny again. At one point in the winter of 1982 we attempted to make arrangements to go back to Hohenwald, Tennessee where my parents were living. However, some of the family members were still so mad at us for leaving the group we were told that they would not be attending the Christmas dinner at our folks house if we were going to be there. We decided to stay away from Hohenwald and give the wound a little more time to heal.

For the longest time I felt so lonely for the company of my childhood playmate that I could hardly stand it. I would literally walk the floor of our newly acquired rental house and pray for reconciliation between us.

Little did I realize at the time, Kenny had slipped into a form of clinical depression. These were difficult times for me but no doubt even more difficult for Kenny. In later years Kenny would explain how lost he felt without his little brother around and how success didn't seem all that important unless I was there to share it with him. Kenny further informed us that during the early eighties he had often gotten so emotionally low that he frequently thought of suicide.

During those lonely times, I kept remembering a prophecy I had been given by a local pastor in Hendersonville, Tennessee, directly before our transition to Oklahoma. "Even as Joseph's brothers came unto him, so will your brothers come to you!" I really could not comprehend what the prophecy could possibly be referring to when I received it. The only thing I knew for certain that made sense in the prophecy was that Joseph's brothers came to him for help in their time of need. My relationship with Kenny and other family members improved slightly over the next several months and after a while, we even felt comfortable enough to attend some of their nearby concerts. They even asked me to join them a couple of times to sing a song I had written in the mid-seventies, entitled "Come To The Water." Even with this tiny bit of interaction, there was still a rather cold distance between me, Kenny and the other members of the group.

By 1984, my reputation as a preacher had spread to many areas across the United States. Jana and I had even released an album the year before and had appeared on both the "PTL Club" and The Trinity Broadcasting Network in Santa Anna, California to promote it. We were ministering that summer in the little town of Stanley, North Carolina, when our phone rang. On the other end of the line, Kenny's voice sounded startled. "Larry?" Kenny asked in a rather cautious tone.

"Kenny?" I responded in an obvious tone of disbelief.

"Larry, we need your help," Kenny went on to explain. "Eric has left us without much notice and we have dates that must be fulfilled. Can you help us?" His question seemed laced with the knowledge that hard feelings had existed between us. I knew that it was a humbling question for him to ask and I made every effort to make it easier.

"Yes Kenny, I'll do it, but I'll have to cancel my next six weeks of engagements."

"Great!" he blurted out. "One other thing," he interjected, "Ronny wants to tell you how much he loves you as well!" Ronny's words were kind and soothing and I knew that truly the worst of times were fully behind us. "One more thing!" Kenny continued, after Ronny gave him back the phone. "Yvonne's going in for some much needed surgery and we were wondering if Jana could sing in her place while you're with us." Once again, his tone sounded apprehensive.

"Sure!" I replied after getting the go ahead signal from Jana. By the time the conversation was concluded there was a total reconciliation between both Kenny and I and the rest of my family. I was on cloud nine just to know that everything was mended and that the prophecy from three years earlier had been fulfilled! Never again would there be a conflict between my brothers and sister and me of such magnitude.

By the time our six weeks were concluded a young man by the name of Billy Ray Brown was working nicely into Eric's old position and Yvonne was back on her feet singing stronger than ever! Jana and I returned to evangelism knowing that we had seen the divine providence of the Lord at work. We were thankful to be in the center of His will.

# CHAPTER THIRTEEN

## A CALL TO PASTOR

In 1986, a third child was born to us. We called him Matthew, as we truly felt him to be a precious gift from God. At this time that Jana and I first starting feeling the Lord tug on our hearts to pastor a church and give our five-member family some much-needed time off from the road. A number of pastoral offers started to pour in from around the nation, and we knew by this sudden surge of invitations that the Lord was confirming our direction in the ministry.

By early 1987 Kenny had finally decided to answer the call of God on his life with regard to preaching the gospel. He sometimes joined Jana and me in between his concert appearances with The Hinsons in order to perform with us as a trio. We usually ministered at a particular church for a couple of services. Normally we sang a few songs and then he or I would preach.

By the spring of 1987, Jana and I came off the road of evangelism to pastor a church in North Little Rock, Arkansas called Capital City Christian Center. That same summer Jana and I invited Kenny to come and join us for a concert at our church. Each time we ministered together during that time the connection between us became more and more powerful. Kenny was truly beginning to hunger after more than just to sing. He wanted to branch out into crusade work throughout the world.

Looking back, I realize that this special time helped to set the stage in our lives for the reunion tour that was to come in 1993 and the church-like atmosphere each one of those concerts possessed. The Hinsons celebrated twenty years in the ministry that year in December of 1987 and I had the privilege to join them for the anniversary concert in Fort Worth, Texas. We repeated the concert the next evening at my church in North Little Rock.

Kenny's personal anointing had increased tremendously by then. I had not seen someone so on fire for God in a very long time. But as I watched Kenny during that particular time I knew his days with the group were numbered.

I invited him to come and hold a couple of meetings for me at my church. His preaching was so incredibly good that you would have thought that he had been preaching for years!

By 1988, Kenny was feeling a strong pull to go into full time evangelism with his personal family. This was a very difficult time of transition for Kenny because he did not want to continue to just sing. He decided that it was necessary to leave the singing group to completely devote his energy to his preaching. Who would have ever guessed that Kenny would follow in his little brother's footsteps?

At one time, he had told the Lord that he couldn't preach and that He should send his little brother Larry instead. "Like with Moses," he told the Lord, "I don't speak as well as my little brother Larry, so send him to preach Your word." During 1988, Kenny wanted to leave the group so badly to preach full time that he could hardly stick around to fulfill the remaining dates in his contract. Kenny called me as often as twice a week in those days. He was either attempting to get my advice on when to leave or sharing something with me that the Lord had spoken to him.

Finally in June of that year Kenny officially performed his last engagement with the Hinsons and the group was formally disbanded. Shortly after Kenny left the group, he jumped into evangelism with both feet.

Kenny and his family often came to spend the night at my house when they passed through on their way to one of their revival meetings. On one particular trip he was scheduled to preach in Humble, Texas just outside Houston. When he passed back through Little Rock on his way back to Nashville, Tennessee, he stopped and stayed overnight with us. That evening he told me that he had enjoyed the revival meetings, although they had been poorly attended. "Larry," he chuckled, "I don't have any ego left." He continued, still laughing over the memory of his most recent encounter. "God has stomped every bid of ego out of me at this past revival."

I looked at him with half a grin on my face and the other half with a curious expression. "The first night of the revival," he continued, "there was a total of eight people in attendance and four of them was me and my family!" Kenny now busted out into a full-fledged laugh. I couldn't help but join him seeing that he was such a major artist in gospel music and no one even showed up to hear him preach.

"Now you know what I felt like the first time you came to hear me preach in Arkansas!" I blurted out, attempting to gain my composer. "Who were the other four people?" I asked giggling.

"The pastor and his family!" Kenny replied, doubling over in laughter. "It grew though!" Kenny paused and pointed his right index upward for emphasis. "By the end of the revival, we had fifteen people in attendance!" The two of us laughed for several minutes until the subject matter slowly changed to a more serious direction. Soon, we were deeply engrossed in the subject of being dedicated to pleasing God, no matter what it takes.

Kenny and I sang together and wept together that night as we spoke of souls coming into the Kingdom of God through the ministries the Lord had given us! I knew then that Kenny had finally discovered the spiritual completion in

## A CALL TO PASTOR

preaching the gospel that he had sought in that little Pentecostal revival we had attended so many years before.

In 1990, Kenny became the pastor of that little Assemblies of God Church where his revival had been so humbling. That same year, I had an overwhelming desire to get the family together for one last recording project. For this reason, I traveled to Nashville in an attempt to get our record producer interested in producing another family project with me included.

That year, I personally struggled with clinical depression as Kenny had before me. Three times I attempted to end my life and yet God miraculously prevented me each time! The Lord sent Kenny to me to talk to me about what he had battled. It was then that I learned that he had felt so low at the time of my departure from the group in 1981 that he too had nearly taken his own life. He told me his feelings one night as we sat in his Cadillac parked in front of a Kroger's food store. He said he felt as if I had actually died the day I left the group to evangelize. He apologized for his hard feelings towards me and his lack of understanding at the time. He told me that he had not known then what God's tug felt like to preach full time.

Admittedly, Kenny's talk didn't seem to help me at the time. Those who struggle with deep depression usually can't hear what a counselor says let alone accept the advice. I was convinced that no one, including Kenny, understood me and that I would be stuck in this dilemma all alone forever. God ultimately delivered me that same year and I continued to pastor and work towards getting a brand new Hinson project recorded.

By 1991, we finally started recording the album I had so diligently striven for. Jana and I made our way to Kenny's house in Houston so that I could work with him on the songs for the upcoming project. Kenny led me into his home office and picked up a box guitar resting in a guitar stand in the corner of the room. He strummed the strings, before taking each key and tuning them separately. "I first heard about

Jesus, sittin' on my mama's knee." The opening line impacted me immediately and I swallowed hard. No sooner had Kenny started to sing his latest song for me than tears began flowing down his cheeks. He paused for a moment and wiped them away with the cuff of his shirtsleeve and then continued singing and playing the rest of the song until by the time he had finished, we were both crying like babies.

"You've got to put that on the album!" I exclaimed in a broken voice, still blowing my nose in a tissue I had retrieved from a tissue box atop Kenny's desk.

"Do you think it's good enough?" Kenny asked with a genuine attitude of concern.

"Good enough?" I responded with an air of disbelief. "It's not only good enough, it ought to be the single!" My exuberance over the number was more than evident and yet Kenny simply played it off as if it was just an all right song. Sometimes the humility that Kenny displayed during that particular time of his life was just plain overwhelming. For that reason I just couldn't imagine how so many individuals with lesser talent than he sometimes acted so arrogant and pompous.

Later that year we met with Ronny and Yvonne in Nashville to rehearse three of the songs we planned to record. We also rehearsed "Joy Comes In The Morning" which I had written and "Sing One More Song About Heaven," which Ronny had written. Finally the song that Kenny sang to me at his home in Houston, "I'll Never Be Over The Hill," was included in our repertoire.

Shortly afterwards we were at Reflections recording studio in Nashville laying down the music and vocal tracks for the first three songs we had rehearsed. Kenny's close friend and co-producer Dirk Johnson joined us on the project for the more difficult and intricate parts of the production. The project seemed to be going so well that we were already making plans to come back as quickly as possible to finish the rest of the album.

Unfortunately, no sooner had we concluded recording of the first three songs than a conflict of contractual agreements brought a screeching halt to any further recording of the project. It would be nearly one year before both the record label and the Hinsons could agree to terms on a new contract.

In the fall of the year, a terrible tragedy struck our family. Our dad Cecil, who was only seventy-six years old, passed away with brain cancer. It was a tremendous blow to the whole family but most of all to our mother Stella. The funeral was so difficult to sing at and yet we felt that it was our final way of honoring the man who had taught us how to have faith in God.

Months afterwards, Kenny and his wife and Jana and I spent several days renovating the interior of Mom's house to help her get past the pain of losing the sweetheart she had loved since she was fifteen years old. Kenny decided to buy her a little miniature poodle and asked me if I would like to share the cost and present the gift to her together. I agreed to do so and Ginger, as Mom came to call her for her auburn coat of fur, is still with her to this very day!

Kenny often referred to the time of Dad's passing as a "glorious homecoming" and "the ultimate healing." He was present at the time of Dad's crossing and felt the presence of the Lord as they sang together with the old man's hands lifted towards heaven in his final praise to God!

Finally in 1992, "The One More Hallelujah" project was finished and released. Ronny suggested that we do a tour with the same name, providing that the response to the project was positive enough. Kenny, Yvonne and I agreed and plans were made to contact Frank Arnold and Brian Hudson to work with us on scheduling and promoting engagements nation wide. In the meantime, Kenny resigned his church in Houston and eventually moved back to his favorite town of Hendersonville, Tennessee. He attempted to pursue a little more producing of custom recording projects for southern gospel groups and he also continued preaching, returning to the field of evangelism.

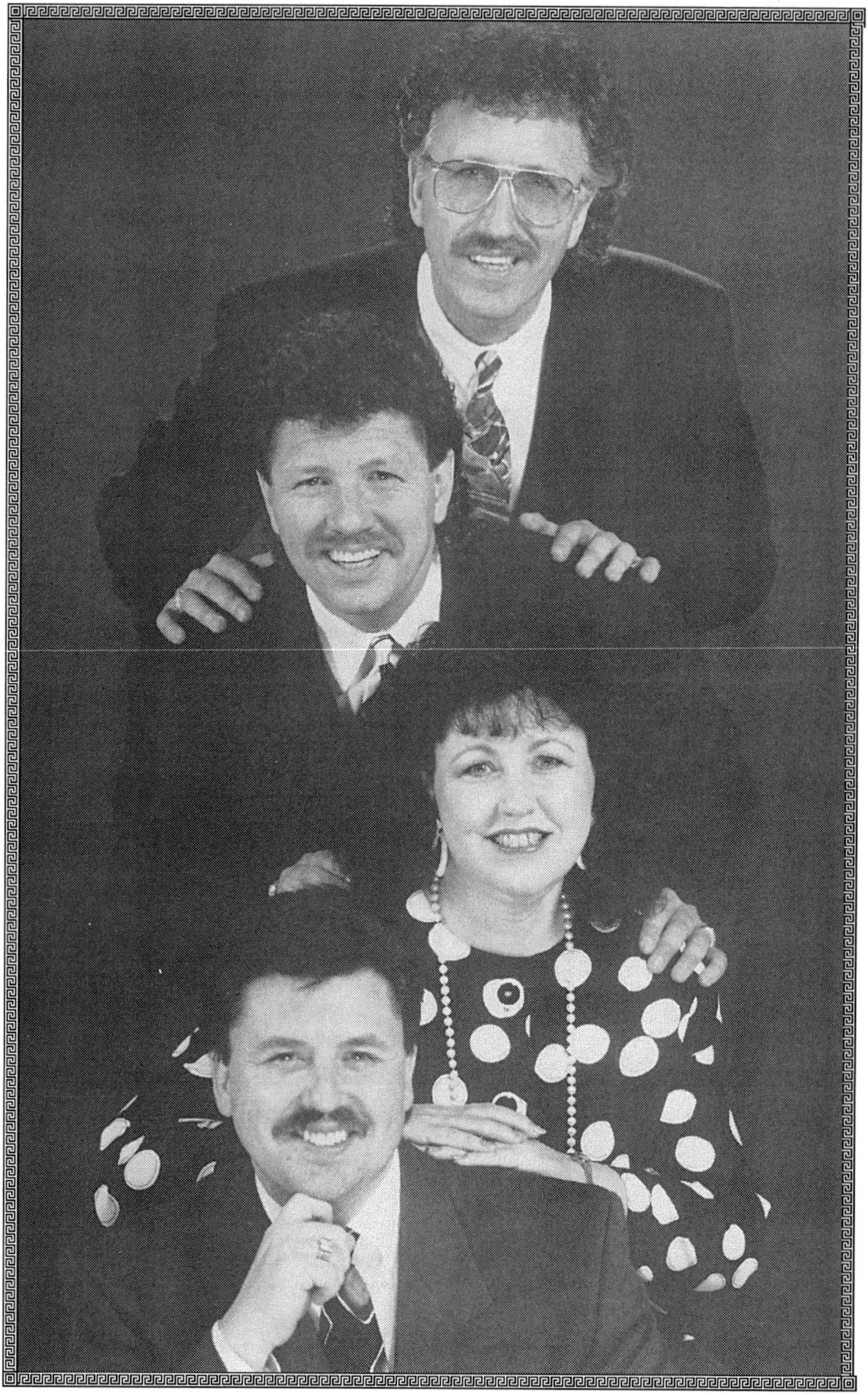

# CHAPTER FOURTEEN

# THE HINSONS MAKE A COME BACK

The spring of 1993 was filled with the evidence of a promising and triumphant return to the field of southern gospel music for the Hinsons.

Although Yvonne was still recuperating from a near fatal car accident of the previous year, everything was now set to go on a reunion tour across America. The Hinsons' newest recording single "Joy Comes In The Morning," was getting excellent chart action in *The Singing News and Voice Magazine*. Thirteen different engagements were scheduled throughout the United States and some autograph parties were arranged at various Christian bookstores in some of the cities where we would be performing.

When our very first weekend of concerts rolled around I rode with our pianist to Nashville where we would rendezvous with the rest of family to drive our leased coach onto West Virginia. After everything was set up on stage and at the record table Kenny confided in me of his concerns with regard to the small crowd in attendance that night. With only minutes left before the concert was to begin Kenny had taken a quick peek at the amount of people present in the concert hall and conferred with Ronny who had just returned from checking on ticket sales. Kenny was troubled by the shortage of interest on the part of gospel music fans.

"Larry?" Kenny asked worriedly.

"Yeah?" I responded not yet knowing what it was that was bothering him.

"Where is everyone?" he asked, cocking his head to the right. I knew that he wasn't really asking me for a definite answer but for more of an educated guess.

"I don't know, Kenny!" I responded, not truly understanding myself the reason only a few people had shown up to hear us sing. "Maybe the promoter didn't get the word out properly," I suggested in a halfhearted manner. "Or maybe, it's a secret singing!"

Kenny immediately started laughing, as he knew too well what a "Secret Singing" was. As a matter of fact, he had coined the phrase himself many years earlier in order to make fun of bogus excuses that promoters sometimes used when they had not used the proper channels to get the word out to the fans.

"That's it!" Kenny said while continuing to laugh. "It's a secret singing!" He emphasized the comment with a nod of his head and the expression of someone who was pleased with himself for solving a very difficult riddle. When the singing began and The Perry Sisters opened the program that evening, Kenny got the group together in one of the dressing rooms for prayer.

Kenny spoke first after praying. "I know that there's not a lot of people out there to sing to tonight, however, that doesn't matter to me any more." He wiped his eyes with a tissue as he continued speaking in a cracking voice. "I didn't come here tonight to put on a show, I came to sing for Jesus!" His demeanor was that of someone who was determined to complete his or her mission, regardless of the obstacles they might encounter along the way. Without exception we all agreed with a loud round of "Amen" and even some hallelujahs. With that, Kenny started a tradition that continued throughout the remainder of the tour. He led us all in a back stage sing-along of the old hymn "Little Is Much, When God Is In It." We transcended from one song to the other, singing and weeping until nearly an hour had passed.

It was now time for us to go on stage and yet most of us could hardly talk for crying so much. Ronny felt it necessary to explain to the audience that we were not currently in the best of voice, due to our previous prayer meeting. Nonetheless, we sang to the best of our ability and the crowd didn't seem to mind the few cracks and pops evident in our singing that night. As a matter of fact, most everyone we spoke to afterwards couldn't recall even hearing any!

As the tour continued, the crowds increased and so did the momentum of the anointing. By the time we reached the Mabee Center at ORU University in Tulsa, Oklahoma, the anointing was so powerful we almost couldn't leave the dressing room where we had been involved with both praise and prayer for at least an hour.

When anyone watches the video of that particular night that Frank Arnold filmed on his personal video camera, one can't help but be overwhelmed by the dynamic preaching that Kenny delivered to the audience. He actually took his Bible in his hand and referenced a scripture about Joshua and the people of Israel choosing whom they would serve. You talk about getting excited! The crowd actually began to sense the anointing on them as well! The whole arena nearly came unglued.

At the conclusion of the service I spoke of my depression and how God had delivered me and how that the Lord could deliver anyone who asked for his touch. Afterwards, Kenny and I prayed with over twenty-five people who had been suffering with deep depression. The two of us would pray for them awhile and then weep with them.

By May of that year, the "One More Hallelujah" tour was becoming such a success that there were plans to extend the tour beyond the summer months. We paused from the tour to attend the National Quartet Convention as it was wrapping up its last year in Nashville. We had a lot of personal and group interviews to grant that year. One in particular with *Voice Magazine* since we were the featured artists on its October cover. We took several photographs with fans and friends and truly enjoyed all the festivities.

About the second night of the convention, Kenny left for home early complaining of being extremely tired. He said that his lower back was aching quite a bit and that he simply needed to go home and rest.

The next evening, Jana and I decided not to go to convention but to spend sometime with an old friend in town. Both Kenny and I had known Rebecca Pruett since she was fourteen years old. At one time, she had even worked as Kenny's personal secretary at Fire Heart Records. She invited us to eat with her and to meet up later with one of her country music friends.

We were at Rebecca's apartment when we got the news that Kenny had to be taken to a hospital emergency room with regard to his lungs. Jana and I quickly rushed from Rebecca's place in Mount Juliet to Kenny' place in Hendersonville. When we arrived, we were informed that the doctors thought he might have pneumonia. Kenny asked if the family would pray for his healing and we gladly complied.

While praying, I felt the spirit of prophecy move upon me and I spoke a word of instruction from the Lord over Kenny. I told Kenny that the illness in his lungs would not lead to death. After leaving their home and heading back to Rebecca's to spend the night, Jana asked me a question. "Why did you say that part about the illness not leading to death?" she said with confusion. "I mean, don't you think that it was a bit much for someone who just has pneumonia?"

Her question made me feel a tiny bit confused as well, however, I just decided that God knew what he had spoken through me and I would leave the explanations up to Him! Soon, further checkups would indicate that Kenny was indeed suffering from something far worse than pneumonia.

# CHAPTER FIFTEEN

## THE LAST PERFORMANCE

According to his x-rays, Kenny was suffering with a kidney that was the size of a football. It was also discovered that he had probably been the victim of kidney cancer for at least three years. His lungs were filled with fluid as a result of the cancer and we were told that Kenny would need to have immediate treatment for his illness. It was discovered later that there were several other cancerous tumors throughout his body as well. He was informed that the kind of cancer he had was tremendously aggressive.

After leaving the church in Houston, Kenny was no longer covered by any health insurance by this time and found himself totally reliant on Tennessee health care system, locally referred to as "Tenn-Care." Kenny was granted an experimental program out of Bethesda Naval Hospital just for the expense of his travels. Even with that, it would cost him thousands of dollars in plane flights back and forth to Maryland. These frequent trips had to be financed by close friends and family. Kenny was subjected to extensive testing at Bethesda and given several powerful drugs that did little to curb the disease or its affects.

Kenny felt extremely weak and the tumors began to eat through some of his bones as well. Naturally all plans were halted for a second leg of the "One More Hallelujah" tour as Kenny resolved to wage a valiant attempt at recovering. Kenny watched and listened to everything pertaining to healing. He even went about his home praying constantly and reading passages of faith and healing from a small booklet he loved to read. Kenny knew in his spirit that God was going to heal him and he openly spoke of being restored and continuing the tour.

In one late night conversation I had with him at his home in Hendersonville, Kenny revealed to me his ministry dreams for the future. "Larry?" Kenny opened the conversation still weeping from the powerful healing video we had just watched on TV together. I lifted my head and looked in his direction and waited for his next words before speaking. "I want to do crusades." His words were somewhat muffled by the handkerchief he was using to cover his mouth and nose.

"Crusades?" I asked, as I wiped the tears away from my eyes.

"Yeah, I want to hold crusades around the world and preach and sing and just allow people to come to God," he continued, blowing his nose into the little white square piece of cloth. I nodded my head in agreement and my tears started flowing freely again. "I want to lay my hands on the sick and crippled and watch God set them free!" He exclaimed standing to his feet and pacing back and forth in front of his fireplace. Earlier that year I had also prophesied to Kenny that there were strong desires in his heart to minister on foreign soil and see the sick and diseased healed. I went further to tell him that the Lord had shown me his wish to be like a certain Assembly of God missionary to India who had witnessed diseases dying in his hand under a microscope. Kenny then informed me that only he and God had known of that secret desire and because of this proof he knew that I was truly speaking for the Lord!

I remember speaking to him by phone while he was still at Bethesda Hospital in Maryland. It was then that he revealed to me that he had been taking such powerful drugs for his cancer that he had been experiencing tormenting dreams. These were dreams he told me where large tumors with long fangs and sharp teeth were attacking him and biting his entire body. He told me that the dreams had repeatedly returned each night and that only recently God had given him a victory after much prayer. He told me that his latest dream had been similar to watching a television program and that as the tumors came to attack him this time, it was as though God turned the channel and he saw he and I in a large crusade ministering to thousands of people!

As 1994 progressed, Kenny continued his treatments both at home and in Maryland. But he also continued to grow weaker. The pain was increasing as well, and his wife often called me in North Little Rock to have me pray with him over the phone for hours until the pain stopped or he simply fell asleep.

As the Quartet Convention drew near that year Kenny prepared to put in an appearance. He had been nominated by *Voice Magazine* for three different categories and was determined to attend the ceremony. He went to the convention that year with his right hand wrapped in a cast where a tumor had eaten through his wrist bone.

At the awards program for *Voice Magazine* Kenny was anxious as it came time to announce the winner for the Living Legend award. I thought he was just feeling butterflies over the anticipation of who would win. However, I soon discovered that this was not his problem at all. After the names of the nominees were announced and as the envelope was about to be opened revealing the winner, Kenny leaned over and whispered in my left ear. "I don't want any sympathy awards and I sure don't want an award that might indicate that I am just a memory of what I once was." I realized then that Kenny still had plenty of plans to beat the cancer and that as far as he was concerned his better days were before him. I couldn't help but smile at his comment.

The fact that he didn't win the award seemed to give him tremendous comfort. "Good," he muttered. He now knew that the gospel music industry did not view him as being all

# THE LAST PERFORMANCE

washed up! Before long the categories switched to Male Vocalist of the Year and Song of the Year. Kenny won in both categories and left that day holding two Diamond Awards that he would later display in his home office next to his vast collection of trophies.

The following evening while enjoying the camaraderie of old friends and fans we received the news that The Hopper Brothers and Connie wanted the Hinsons to join them on stage for a special tributary song. So right in the middle of their performance of "The Lighthouse" the Hoppers introduced the Hinsons to the jammed packed arena in Louisville, Kentucky. The entire audience seemed to explode with excitement as Kenny, still brandishing his white cast, began the first verse of the legendary number singing in his well-known country gospel style voice. I had never been as proud of Kenny as I was that very moment on stage before the massive crowd of fans and I will always been grateful to the Hoppers for allowing him his final hour in the spotlight!

The anointing came over him so dramatically that night that he told me how he was completely painless during the entire performance. The anointing lingered afterwards as well and he spoke of his complete recovery and how God had shown him what the day would be like when he would ultimately be delivered from cancer! He also spoke of feeling strong enough to continue the tour. He felt as though his condition was going to turn around very soon.

Unfortunately, Kenny got even weaker after that appearance and though he continued to try and preach for a while the disease and the medical treatments finally drained him of all his ability to travel or minister. By the spring of 1995, Kenny was growing increasingly worse and was forced to go back to Summit Hospital in Nashville. Suddenly, we found ourselves in the fight of our lives as we attempted to help Kenny meet the overwhelming challenge that lay just ahead.

# CHAPTER SIXTEEN

# THE LEGEND HAS PASSED

Kenny remained unbelievably positive in his attitude throughout the long process of his illness. For this reason he wanted absolutely no one around him but those who spoke in faith with regard to his total recovery. He was not going to speak negatively and he refused to entertain the company of anyone out side of close family and friends that also spoke positive words of faith and scripture over him!

We decided that unless we were one hundred percent certain that someone who had come to visit him was positive in their confession of faith they were not allowed any access or contact with him, in any way. Some people could not understand this and immediately became emotionally hurt or angry when they had driven to see him or wanted to go up to his room and pray for him. Nonetheless, these were Kenny's wishes and we fully intended to secure them. After all, he was the one in a literal fight for his life and he possessed the right to call the shots as to his own psychological and spiritual needs at the time.

"Larry?" Kenny asked weakly, as he pushed himself up to sit on the edge of his hospital bed at Summit. "I want you to come into an agreement with me, a covenant. If I should I get to death's door don't let me go through it!" He reached his hand over and placed it on the back of my hand to emphasize the agreement and to remind me that he was counting on me.

"Okay," I agreed as I pondered the struggle that no doubt lay before us.

"Bring everyone into agreement for my healing and don't allow them to speak death over me, only healing!"

"All right," I said, nodding my head simultaneously. "I'll do it Kenny!"

Kenny closed his eyes and lay back on the hospital bed again to rest. I stood to leave the room trying to be as quiet in my departure as possible. Just as I was about to step over the threshold of the doorway leading to the hospital corridor, Kenny called my name a second time. "Larry?" Kenny whispered. "You always were my little giant." I felt my reply catch in my throat, as tears flooded my eyes. Finally, I was able to respond, though I did so softly. "You'll always be my hero, Kenny."

I took the elevator to the first level and went directly to the hospital prayer chapel. Many of our close family members and friends had been taking turns there at the twenty-four hour prayer meetings we held constantly during Kenny's illness. Many times the singing emanating from the little chapel would attract hospital staff members and strangers who had come to work or to visit sick relatives. They would suddenly drop in for prayer and to bask in the presence of almighty God. At one time, some strangers were even being slain under the power of the Holy Spirit upon being prayed for.

On several occasions the fire alarm went off and the fire doors would shut, as we opened the door of the chapel after one of our many heated prayer meetings. As I opened the door of the prayer chapel this time to convey Kenny's latest wish to the faithful few, I briefly interrupted their prayers to share with them what Kenny had instructed me to do. As I disclosed Kenny's deepest desires to the little group of people in the cramped chamber I had each one of them take their neighbor's hand. I then asked each of them to come into agreement with Kenny and me. In essence, I informed them that they were about to enter a covenant relationship with Kenny and that if they were not entirely certain that they would be able to speak positively and in faith they should not participate in this act of agreement. Without exception, everyone inside the tiny chapel held hands and took a vow to believe for Kenny's healing and to only speak words of blessing and healing over his life.

Unfortunately, it didn't take long until a few people began to break that covenant. Some even started speaking about making funeral arrangements and what they should wear at the funeral. We were quite aware of the fact that many people were starting to show signs of fatigue as a result of the many long hours involved in wagging the on-going battle. Yet, no one, outside of his wife, was more exhausted than Yvonne, Ronny and our Mama. They had all spent countless hours at Kenny's bedside. Jana I had spent a great deal of money and time on the road traveling back and forth between North Little Rock and Nashville and even staying sometimes in motels. We ate the majority of our meals with the rest of the family in the McDonald's restaurant built onto the hospital's lobby, and we were as tired of the struggle as anyone was.

For this reason, we truly believed that weariness was no excuse for throwing in the towel at this stage of the game. The more invested, the more you should plan to stick it out for the long haul. At least that's how Jana and I saw it. Thank God for people like Roy and Ann Chapman, close friends of Kenny's and former board members in his Houston church. They and their daughter Deanna stood with us in prayer consistently throughout the entire ordeal. They were part of the very few that joined Ronny, Harold, Yvonne, Jana and me in those twenty-four hour prayer vigils.

A few times when we received some discouraging news about Kenny's progression, Roy was one of the people that went up to his room with me to lay hands on him with a heavy anointing from time to time. Altogether the entire prayer group was successful in helping Kenny returned from death's door approximately seven different times!

There were many times when Jana and I were barely awake as we took our turn at watching over him as he slept. Once Jana had just cracked a private joke when Kenny made a snorting noise that served to wake him up. Even in his sedated frame of mind he still managed to maintain his personal dignity. When he inadvertently woke himself at the moment of our laughter over Jana's little joke, he immediately thought we were laughing at him. He asked the question in a muffled tone from behind the clear oxygen mask over his face. "What? What did I do?" Jana and I admittedly lost it for a moment, as we could not help but burst into laughter over Kenny's untimely inquiry. We finally managed to convince him of the true reason for our humorous outburst and he eventually drifted back to sleep again.

At one point, we received word from one of Kenny's doctors that he had an inoperable tumor wrapped around his spinal cord. This particular tumor made it impossible for Kenny to feel his legs and feet let alone do any walking. There were several other tumors in Kenny's body at this phase in his battle with cancer, including in one of his intestines. A former nurse's aid warned us that Kenny was considered a terminal patient and that we should be careful to not allow them to increase his oxygen all the way up and then heavily sedate him. According to the aid, such a combination was a common practice in hospitals where a patient who was labeled terminal and was on a state health care program was concerned. "Just remember!" He told us. "One hundred percent oxygen and heavy sedation will throw him into pneumonia. He'll go comatose and die." His words were both sobering and deeply appreciated.

We continued to diligently maintain a constant prayer chain and Kenny gradually began to improve in many different areas. We don't exactly know what happened to the inoperable tumor that had been wrapped around Kenny' spine, however, he began to feel his legs and feet again! He even managed to walk some with the aid of a walker. Kenny continued to maintain his faith and positive confession as well. When someone would ask him if he still believed God for his complete recovery, Kenny would often respond by saying, "He's never failed me yet!"

Once he told me in private, "Larry, I love my kids so much that I've got to live in order to see them grow up!" All the Hinson family, without exception, believed that Kenny would never do anything but live to declare the works of the Lord!

Jana and I went back to North Little Rock for a short time before the tragic end began to unexpectedly unfold. Kenny's wife became so exhausted that she too had to be placed in the hospital for stress related problems. In the meantime, we suspect that the already reluctant medical board providing Kenny's health care decided to suspend any further treatments for cancer. They clearly considered him well beyond his terminal budget.

Mama, Yvonne, Ronny and several other family members as well as some close friends left the hospital to get something to eat. When they left, Kenny was on approximately seven-percent oxygen and very little medication. To the family, this was a sure sign of his recovery. Nonetheless, we were also aware of the fact that some of the doctors had tried to intimidate Kenny's wife into allowing him to die with, as they put it, "Dignity"!

When the family returned from dinner and Wal-Mart only a few hours later, they discovered Kenny in a painful condition. Our worst nightmare had been realized. They also discovered that soon after they left for dinner, someone increased his pain medication inducing a deep sleep and also increased his oxygen to one hundred percent. By the time we got the news of his condition and drove the five hours to Nashville, Kenny was already in the Critical Care Unit.

Debbie invited Jana and me in first along with our mother. I looked closely at the heart monitor as I approached the right side of his bed behind the drawn curtains. As I started to speak to him, I watched his heart rate increase dramatically and I knew that he could hear me. I spoke the familiar words in his left ear as I began intensely praying for him to come out of his coma. Words that I had spoken over him so many times before and that he had always responded excellently to. "Man of God, rise up in the name of Jesus." The heart rate monitor unquestionably indicated that the words were stirring faith inside both his mind and his spirit. The more I prayed, the stronger his heart rate became.

Soon, his children, Amanda, who was then sixteen years old, and Weston, only eleven at the time, entered the room and approached either side of his bed. As they spoke to him and reassured him of their love and prayers, again the heart monitor showed apparent signs of his awareness. Jana and I continued praying hard for his recovery and continued to witness the change in his heart rate during prayer. I kept remembering what he said to me prior to the covenant I had made with him to always stay positive. "I'm may get to death's door, but don't let me go through it!"

For this reason, I prayed even more intensely. I refused to back off, thinking that this was what Kenny had warned me about. However, somewhere around 5:20 on the evening of July 27, 1995, I distinctly heard the voice of the Lord tell me to speak these words in his ear: "The decision is up to you as to whether you live or go to be with the Lord." I did not want to obey what I was hearing and did my best to ignore it as unbelief and surrender on my part. Yet, the Lord spoke a second time and repeated the same statement.

You may be someone who chooses to believe that God doesn't speak to people that way in contemporary times like these. Yet, when I told Kenny it was his decision and not mine, his heart rate dropped immediately and he died within approximately five minutes. Even at that, I did not want to release him to heaven and being somewhat confused as to my role in bringing him back from death's door, I started wondering if I should continue to pray for his resurrection. I called the prayer group together for prayer, just to be certain that we had done everything we knew to do.

After a little while, arrangements were made to have his body prepared for his funeral at Robinson's Funeral Home in Hendersonville.

"Oh, God!" I thought, "my brother and playmate is gone!" What would I do now? Never again, would I have the joy of hearing his voice either in conversation or in song. No longer would I be able to joke with him over childhood personalities we often imitated. My world seemed shattered, and all I wanted to do was cry. My hero, a genuine legend in gospel music, was dead.

When the funeral was scheduled for Christ Church in Nashville, we asked Bo Hinson to sing a song with us that Ronny and Kenny had written during the days of Kenny's last hospital stay. It was probably the hardest thing that any of us had ever undertaken at the time. We sang with cracking voices as tears rushed down our faces and the realization that we would never again stand with him on stage to sing. The casket was closed so that friends and fans alike would remember him the way the picture on his coffin portrayed him, and not like the man the cancer treatments had made him.

After we laid Kenny to rest at what was then called Woodlawn Cemetery in Hendersonville, I fell into a very deep depression. I blamed myself for falsely prophesying early on that Kenny's problem in his lungs would not lead to death. I fully intended to go back to North Little Rock and resign my pastoral as I felt myself unfit to hear from God or to lead his people in the right spiritual direction for their lives. Only through the prayers and assistance of close friends and family around me was I finally able to understand what God was really saying.

He first caused me to realize that I did not truly understand His promises towards His people. He then took me to clear scriptural proof with regard to His will versus man's will. He showed me the passage in I Kings 8:56.

"Blessed be the Lord that has given rest unto his people Israel, according to all that he promised. There hath not failed one word of all his good promise, which he promised by the hand of Moses his servant." This particular passage seems to bear witness of the fact that God promised to not only lead the children out of Egypt by the hand of Moses, but that Moses was to lead them into their inheritance of the Promised Land as well. The only problem with this particular scripture seemed to lie in the fact that Moses didn't actually lead them into the Promised Land. According to Numbers 20:11-12, Moses struck the rock when God told him to speak to it. As a result, Moses did not lead them into the Promised Land, but instead died in the wilderness. God buried him in a secret location.

It was after reading these passages carefully and fully analyzing both their contents and definitions that I felt that God revealed to me the understanding of my prophecy to Kenny and the mystery of his untimely passing. God spoke to my heart the following statements and questions. "Although I instructed Moses to lead the children of Israel into the land that flowed with milk and honey, ultimately Moses did not go in. Tell me now, did I lie?" For a moment, I was stunned at what He had spoken. I attempted to disregard it as a mere psychological means by which to divert the blame from myself. However, the voice of the Lord in my spirit spoke again! "Tell me, did I lie to Moses?" Eventually, I told the lord I didn't know for sure how to answer the question and that He would have to help me see what He was trying to show me.

When the Lord spoke again, I truly understood that His ways are above my ways and that His thoughts are genuinely above my thoughts. "When I give someone a promise," the Lord continued. " I give it to them on a contingency basis. I choose to allow men and women to hear the good news of what will transpire in their lives, providing that they will to enact my will." The Lord's words were flowing rapidly into my own spirit now and I could feel His peace beginning to overtake me. "It was my will to have Moses lead the Israelites into the Promised Land and when I told him he would lead them in, I spoke to him of my will, not of his will." Then the Lord explained even further. "Moses had every provision for entering the land of promise, but he chose not to do so by means of disobedience." His methods of operation were becoming even clearer to me, the longer He spoke. "Kenny knew that my will for his future was to live and minister my gospel." As the Lord spoke even more, tears began running down my cheeks. "Kenny possessed a will as well as Moses and I allowed him to choose to either live there with you or to live here with me. His choice was not one of disobedience as with Moses, however, all my promises depend upon one's willingness to fulfill them." His final words are stamped upon my heart forever. "I let Kenny choose, remember?"

At this writing, it has been over eight years since his passing and yet I still remember his laugh, his wit, his talent and his anointing. I sometimes cry when I'm alone. Not because I'm uncertain of his whereabouts, no, I cry for me and for his children. I cry for his siblings and for his eighty two year old mother. I cry because we miss him so terribly and long for the day of the Lord's return so that we might hold him in our arms again. So that we might hear what angels are hearing right this moment--that incomparable sound that for a brief time touched so many lives and made them sing, too!

Recently, I pictured myself long ago in that little community of Aromas. It seemed like only yesterday that Kenny climbed aboard that big yellow school bus as I peered after him on my tiptoes through the large bay window of our house. I always knew back then that at some point in the day he would return to join me again and we would frolic away the hours until the afternoon sun began to hide its light from the night. This time I know that the bus will not come at the end of the day. At least, it won't come at the end of some normal day. But one day it will come. And when it comes, we

## THE LEGEND HAS PASSED

will see and hear Kenny sing again, and this time the legend will live in our midst forever! I suppose that my personal message to him, I had written on his wreath card at his viewing, says it best, "I will sing with you again at the resurrection, you take the lead."

Kenny-age 4¹/². Larry - age 2

The Hinsons 1969

Early Hinson Apperance on the
"Gospel Singing Jubilee."

Kenny and Larry
(Front yard of 354 Berry Road
Los Lomas, CA)

Kenny in front of our bus in 1970.

1967 Photo session in our home at Berry Road.

1969 in our living room at Berry Road.

Kenny poses with mom.

Larry and Kenny on dad's car with tennis ball under Larry's sleeve in 1966.

Kenny and Larry in dad's cornfield, next to the shed where they saw the devil.

The Revengers
(Kurt, Larry and Kenny)

Yvonne, Kenny and Larry peering over the window pain in Aromas.

Kenny and Larry on tricycles
(Kenny 6, Larry 4)

The Original Hinsons with older brother Harold top left and dad in 1959.

Trip to Mama's birthplace in Big Flat, Arkansas, 1969.

Kenny at Band apartment in Madisonville, KY 1973.

Kenny in Bahamas August 1974.

Haunted church on Zoe Street, Houston, Texas 1970.

Icecycles dripping on Yvonne, Kenny and Larry Aromas, CA 1962.

The Hinsons with Chris Hawkins aboard the S.S. Bahamas Star 1974.

Kenny with his children he adored, Amanda and Weston.

The Hinsons on back of flat bed truck in 1973.

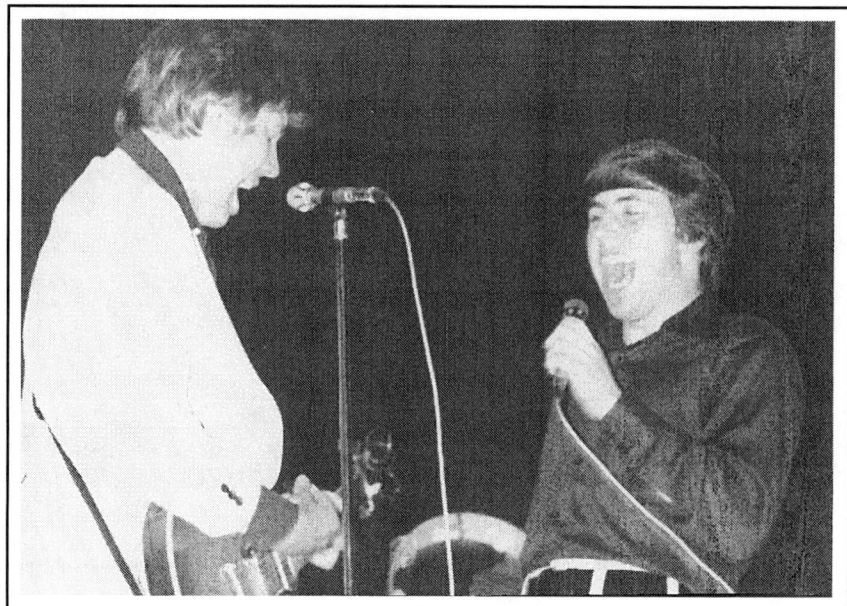

1974 Kenny and Larry singing, "Ain't that what it's all about."

Larry and Kenny clowning around during Christmas 1979.

Kenny 1979 in the roll of blind justice.

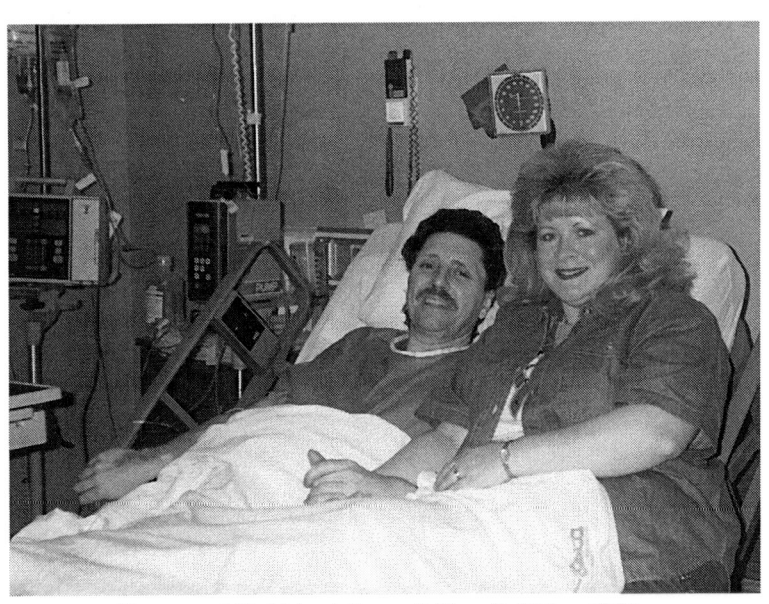

Kenny and Debbie at Summit Hospital May 1995.

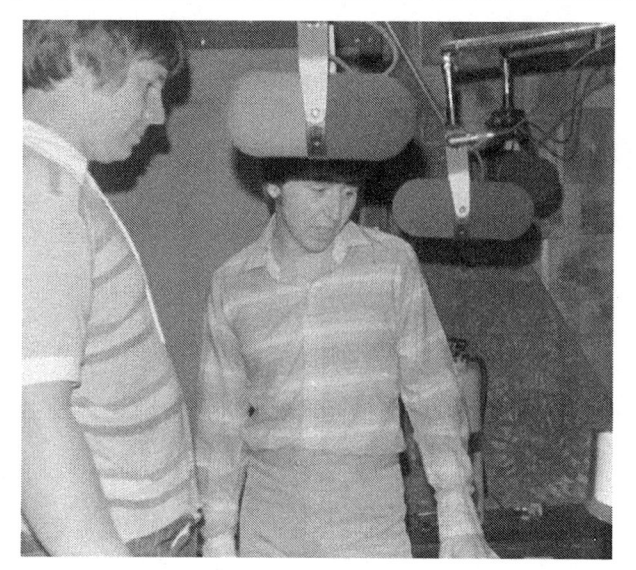

Kenny and Larry in Hilltop recording studio Nashville, TN 1977.

The Original Hinsons autograph and live radio party, North Little Rock, Arkansas, during the One More Hallelujah tour in 1993.

Kenny arrives in Bethesda, Maryland for surgery 1993.

Some of Kenny's awards in his office in Hendersonville, Tennessee.

Kenny, Larry and Jana sing together in
North Little Rock, Arkansas in 1987.